On Point
Beginner's English

Student's Book
+ AUDIOS and VIDEOS ONLINE

Cathy and Louis Rogers

1st edition 1 4 3 2 | 2024 23 22

The last figure shown denotes the year of impression.

All rights reserved. No part of this publication may be reproduced, stored in a retrieval system, or transmitted, in any form or by any means, electronic, mechanical, photocopying, recording, or otherwise, without prior written permission from the publisher.

Delta Publishing, 2021
www.deltapublishing.co.uk
www.klett-sprachen.de/delta

© Ernst Klett Sprachen GmbH, Rotebühlstraße 77, 70178 Stuttgart, 2021

Editor: Sheila Dignen
Advisers: Liz Foody, Sarah Walker
Layout and typesetting: Wild Apple Design Ltd.
Cover: Andreas Drabarek, Wild Apple Design Ltd.
Cover picture: Getty Images (Martin Barraud), Munich
Printing and binding: Elanders GmbH, Waiblingen

ISBN 978-3-12-501265-3

This book contains audios, videos and flash cards available on the DELTA Augmented app.

| Download the free DELTA Augmented app onto your device | Start picture recognition and scan the pages with this symbol or audio/video icons | Download files and use them now or save them for later |

Apple and the Apple logo are trademarks of Apple Inc., registered in the US and other countries. App Store is a service mark of Apple Inc. | Google Play and the Google Play logo are trademarks of Google LLC.

On Point

On Point is a modern course with new and innovative topics, but it is also traditional in its approach. With a clear structure and careful progression, we're sure you will sense your progress as you enjoy working through the course.

Lessons A and B
Lessons A and B are the main lessons for grammar. Presented via listening or reading texts, all of the grammar is then analysed and practised before you produce it in an authentic situation. Lessons A and B also present relevant vocabulary for each topic and practise any necessary pronunciation points.

Lesson C
The last lesson in each unit is divided into two halves. The first page presents a set of phrases or a language point that is useful for a particular speaking context. The second page follows a guided approach to help improve your writing skills.

Video Pages
After every two units there is a two-page video lesson related to one of the themes from the previous lessons. The structure of these lessons allows further listening and reading practice. There is also a short review of the main language points covered in the previous two units.

The app
DELTA Augmented lets you play all the audio files, videos and flash cards via the app for free. Simply download the app onto your device and scan the pages with the audio (▶ 000), video (▶) or flash cards icon (📖). Save the files onto your device to use them wherever and whenever you want.

Appendix
The back of the book contains an extended Grammar Reference for you to learn further details of each grammar point. There is also an Irregular Verb list to help you remember these tricky forms as well as pair work speaking files for some of the lessons.

Contents

	Grammar	Vocabulary	Reading / Listening	Speaking / Writing
1 Hello! 1A Hello and goodbye **p6** 1B Introductions **p8** 1C Personal information **p10**	*Be*: I, you, he, she, it	Days Countries **Pronunciation:** Word stress The alphabet Numbers 1 – 20	Saying hello and goodbye Introductions	Personal information
2 Conversations 2A Who are they? **p12** 2B All about you **p14** 2C Everyday conversations **p16**	*Be*: all forms Questions **Pronunciation:** Intonation in questions	Nationalities **Pronunciation:** Word stress Jobs Numbers 21 – 100 Activities	Conversations	Everyday phrases A personal profile
Video: All about me **p18**				
3 Things 3A My things **p20** 3B Shopping **p22** 3C Out and about **p24**	Singular and plural nouns; *a / an / some* **Pronunciation:** plurals *This, that, these, those*	My things Clothes Colours	Shopping	Prices In a café A form Capital letters
4 People and places 4A Family and friends **p26** 4B My home and my things **p28** 4C A night out **p30**	Possessives Adjectives *Have, has*	Family Adjectives for people Adjectives for places and things	A blog **Pronunciation:** 's My brother and sister What's new?	Talking about time Someone in my family Adverbs
Video: Family tree **p32**				
5 My life 5A Activities **p34** 5B Chatting **p36** 5C Talking about yourself **p38**	Present Simple: positive and negative *I, you, we, they* Present Simple questions *I, you, we, they*	Sport and free time Common verbs and nouns together	Activities Conversations	Making small talk *Wh-* questions A blog *And / because*
6 Routines 6A My routine **p40** 6B When do you … ? **p42** 6C In a hotel **p44**	Adverbs of frequency **Pronunciation:** /s/ and /z/; Missing sounds Present Simple: *he, she, it* **Pronunciation** third person *-s*	Verbs for daily routines Prepositions	Mark's Mondays How famous people start the day Questions and answers	Checking in to a hotel Asking about facilities Filling in a form Dates, postcodes and phone numbers
Video: Two different routines **p46**				

4

Contents

	Grammar	Vocabulary	Reading / Listening	Speaking / Writing
7 Free time 7A What do you like doing? p48 7B My favourites p50 7C Travel p52	Like / love / hate + -ing Word order in questions **Pronunciation**: 'Do you' in questions	Free time activities Travel	My friends #metime An interview	At the train station A description of a day Time sequencers
8 Eat, play, shop 8A The food I like p54 8B Yes, I can! p56 8C Making requests p58	Some and any Can and can't	Food **Pronunciation**: sounds and spelling Adverbs	What food do you like? Famous people and food My daughter – the art student Questions and answers	Shopping A text message Making requests and giving answers

Video: Food around the world p60

	Grammar	Vocabulary	Reading / Listening	Speaking / Writing
9 Out and about 9A What are they doing? p62 9B Now and usually p64 9C Meeting up p66	Present Continuous Present Continuous and Present Simple	Verb + noun collocations Holidays and activities **Pronunciation**: word stress	A phone call home A break from normal life	Meeting friends Social media posts
10 Places 10A Holiday rentals p68 10B Where were you? p70 10C A new place p72	There is / There are Was / were	Rooms Places in a town Prepositions	Describing a holiday rental Where were you last night?	Asking for and giving directions An email Describing your home and where it is

Video: Hotels and holidays p74

	Grammar	Vocabulary	Reading / Listening	Speaking / Writing
11 Last week 11A Last weekend p76 11B My best experience p78 11C What was it like? p80	Past Simple: Common irregular verbs Past simple: Regular **Pronunciation**: Past Simple endings	Phrases with do, go, get and have Adjectives to describe experiences	What did you do on Sunday? My experiences abroad My best experiences	Giving opinions **Pronunciation**: showing feelings A restaurant review Describing your experiences
12 Plans and experiences 12A Future plans p82 12B Weekends p84 12C Goodbye and thank you p86	Be going to Pronunciation: weak form of 'to' Tense review	Phrases with do, get, go and move Adjectives to describe feelings	A radio advert What next? Living for the weekend	Starting and ending a conversation Messages Looking back and looking forward

Video: What did you do? p88

Grammar Reference **p90** Communication bank **p98** Irregular verbs **p106** Audio Scripts **p107**

5

1 Hello!

> **Listening:** *Saying hello and goodbye*
> **Vocabulary:** *Days*

1A Hello and goodbye

1 ▶ 001 Read and listen.

Hello. I'm Sam. What's your name?

2 ▶ 001 Listen again and repeat.

3 Stand up and practise. Use your name.

*Hello. I'm ……………………….
What's your name?*

My name's ……………………….

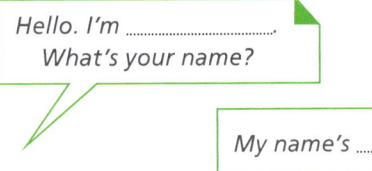

4 ▶ 002 Read and listen.

Hannah:	Hi, Tom. How are you?
Tom:	Fine, thanks, Hannah. And you?
Hannah:	I'm fine, thanks.
Susie:	Hello, Jack. How are you?
Jack:	I'm very well, thanks. And you?
Susie:	I'm OK, thanks.

5 ▶ 002 Listen again and repeat.

6 Work with a partner. Practise the conversations. Use your names.

7 003 Read and listen.

8 003 Listen again and repeat.

9 004 Listen and repeat the days.

WORK DIARY

- Monday
- Tuesday
- Wednesday
- Thursday
- Friday
- Saturday
- Sunday

10 005 Listen and say the next day.

1 Friday

11 Write the days of the week.
1 Today ....
2 Tomorrow ....
3 The weekend .... and ....

12 Practise with a partner.

13 Work with a partner. Complete the three conversations.

See you on Sunday.
My name's Nick.
Goodbye. See you then.
And you?
I'm fine, thanks.

A Hello. My name's George. What's your name?
1 ....

B Hi, Ben. How are you?
I'm very well, thanks.
2 ....
3 ....

C Bye, Anna.
4 ....
5 ....

14 Practise with a partner. Use your names.

1B Introductions

> ▶ **Grammar:** *Be: I, you, he, she, it*
> ▶ **Vocabulary:** *Countries*
> ▶ **Listening:** *Introductions*
> ▶ **Pronunciation:** *Word stress on countries*

1 🔊 006 Listen and read. Then listen and repeat.

Where are you from?

I'm from Brazil.

2 Match the countries to the pictures.

Brazil   Germany   Japan   the USA

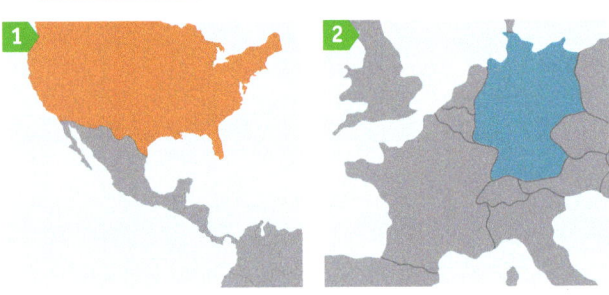

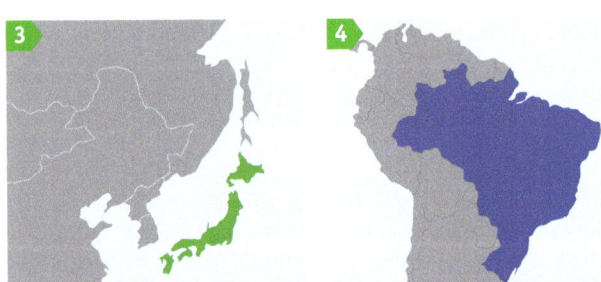

3 🔊 007 Listen and match the person with the country and city.

1	Meiko	Brazil	Berlin
2	Tim	Germany	Frankfurt
3	Ana	Japan	Tokyo
4	Fred	the USA	Osaka
			São Paulo
			Rio de Janeiro
			New York
			San Francisco

4 🔊 008 Read and listen to the countries.

🇧🇷 <u>Bra</u>zil   🇨🇳 <u>Chi</u>na   🇮🇹 <u>I</u>taly
🇫🇷 <u>France</u>   🇲🇽 <u>Mex</u>ico   🇨🇦 <u>Ca</u>nada
🇦🇺 Aus<u>tra</u>lia   🇯🇵 Ja<u>pan</u>

5 🔊 008 Look at the <u>underlined</u> stress on the countries. Listen again and repeat.

6 🔊 009 Choose the correct words. Then listen and check.

A: Hello, I ¹ *'m / are* Michael. What's your name?
B: Hi, I ² *'m / are* Meiko.
A: Nice to meet you.
B: Nice to meet you, too.
A: Where ³ *are / am* you from, Meiko?
B: I ⁴ *'m / are* from Japan.
A: Oh, ⁵ *am / are* you from Tokyo?
B: No, I ⁶ *aren't / 'm not*. I'm from Osaka.

7 Complete the grammar box with *'m* and *are*.

Grammar: *Be: I* and *you*   ▶ PAGE 90

Positive
I ¹ .... / I am from Japan.
You're / You are from Spain.

Negative
I'm not / I am not from Colombia.
You aren't / You are not from here.

Questions
Where ² .... you from?
³ .... you from Sydney?
Where **am** I?   **Am** I right?

Short answers
Yes, **I am**.   Yes, **you are**.
No, I' ⁴ .... not.   No, **you aren't**.

Don't use contractions in positive short answers.
~~Yes, I'm.~~

8

Hello!

8 🔊 010 Complete the conversation. Then listen and check.

am   are   are you (x 2)   I   'm not   I'm   'm   'm

A: Hi, I **¹** 'm Luca.
B: Hi, **²** .... 'm Maria.
A: **³** .... you from Spain?
B: No, I **⁴** .... **⁵** .... from Portugal.
A: Where in Portugal?
B: I **⁶** .... from Porto. Where **⁷** .... from?
A: I'm from England.
B: **⁸** .... from London?
A: Yes, I **⁹** ....

9 Work with a partner. Ask and answer the questions.

10 🔊 011 Listen and read. Write the countries.

1 **A:** This is Justin Bieber.
   B: Where is he from?
   A: He's from **¹** ....

2 **A:** This is Rihanna.
   B: Is she from **²** .... ?
   A: No, she isn't. She's from Saint Michael. It's in **³** ....

11 Complete the grammar box.

Grammar: Be: he, she, it   ▶ PAGE 90

Positive
He's / He **¹** .... from Canada.
She's / She **²** .... from Barbados.
It's / It **³** .... from Canada.

Negative
He **⁴** .... / He is not from Spain.
She **⁵** .... / She is not from Spain.
It **⁶** .... / It is not from Spain.

Questions and short answers
⁷ .... he from Italy? Yes, he **⁸** .... / No, he **⁹** ....
Is she from Canada? Yes, she is. / No, she isn't.

12 Complete the conversations with *is*, *'s* or *isn't*.

1

Name:	Teresa
City:	Faro
Country:	Portugal

A: **¹** .... Teresa from Spain?
B: No, she **²** .... She **³** .... from Portugal.

2

Name:	Yuki
City:	Kyoto
Country:	Japan

A: Yuki is from Kyoto.
B: Where **⁴** .... Kyoto? **⁵** .... it in Japan?
A: Yes, it **⁶** ....

3

Name:	Mario
City:	San Diego
Country:	The USA

A: **⁷** .... Mario from Brazil?
B: No, he **⁸** .... He **⁹** .... from the USA.

13 Create a new person. Write a name, a country and a city from that country.

Name:	....
City:	....
Country:	....

14 Introduce yourself to your partner. Ask questions.

> Hi, my name's Lia.

> I'm Sam. Where are you from, Lia?

15 Work with a partner. Move around the class. Say hello. Then introduce your partner. Ask questions.

> Hi, I'm Lia. And this is Juan. He's from Mexico.

1C Personal information

▸ The alphabet
▸ Numbers 1–20
▸ Phone numbers
▸ Checking information

1 ▶ 012 Listen and read.

2 ▶ 013 Listen and repeat the letters.

3 ▶ 013 Listen again and write the letters in the box in the group with the same sound.

    d g j k l n t u y z

1 a h ..j.. ....
2 b c .... e .... p v
3 f .... m .... s x ....
4 i ....
5 o
6 q .... w
7 r

4 ▶ 014 Listen and check. Then listen again and repeat.

5 ▶ 015 Listen and write the names.

1

First name ....
Surname   ....

2

First name ....
Surname   ....

6 Student A turn to page 98. Student B turn to page 102.

7 ▶ 016 Listen to the numbers and repeat.

  1   2   3   4   5   6   7
  8   9   10 11 12 13 14
  15 16 17 18 19 20

Hello!

8 ▶ 017 Listen and write the numbers.
- a 7
- b
- c
- d
- e
- f
- g
- h
- i
- j

9 ▶ 018 Listen and say the next number.
1 one, two, ...
> three

10 ▶ 019 Read the *Key Language* box. Listen and complete the phone numbers.
1 07............... 65428............... ....
2 .... 286 5............... 734
3 00............... 12............... .... 86...............
.... 45

KEY LANGUAGE Saying phone numbers

07996542831
- oh seven double nine six five four two eight three one

0044 1249863745
- double oh double four one two four nine eight six three seven four five

What's your phone number?

It's 07886 685 923.

11 Write a phone number. Work in pairs. Ask for your partner's phone number and write it.

My phone number ....
My partner's phone number ....

12 ▶ 020 Listen. Then complete the conversations.

| how | name | number | say | ~~what~~ |

1
A: ¹ **What** 's your ² ....?
B: It's Ben Patterson.
A: ³ .... do you spell that?
B: p-a-t-t-e-r-s-o-n

2
A: What's your phone ⁴ ....
B: It's 07992 543 675.
A: Can you ⁵ .... that again, please?
B: Sure. It's 07992 543 675.

13 Complete the *Key Language* box.

KEY LANGUAGE checking information

What's your name?
¹ .... do you spell that?
What's your phone number?
Can you say that ² ....?

14 Work with a partner. Practise the conversations in exercise 12.

15 Work in groups of four. Ask and answer questions to complete the table.

	Student 1	Student 2	Student 3
First name			
Surname			
Phone number			

2 Conversations

- **Vocabulary:** Nationalities
- **Reading:** A blog
- **Pronunciation:** Word stress
- **Grammar:** Be: all forms

2A Who are they?

1 ▶ 030 Listen and read. Complete the sentences with the countries in the box.

> Spain   China   Italy   Scotland

1 His name is Sam. He's from .... He's Scottish.
2 Her name is Ana. She's from .... She's Spanish.

3 It's from .... It's Italian.
4 They're from .... They're Chinese.

2 ▶ 031 Listen and repeat the countries and nationalities.

3 ▶ 031 Listen again. Underline the word stress in the nationalities.

4 Work with a partner. Cover the words for countries and nationalities. Look at the flags. Take turns to say a country and nationality.

	COUNTRY	NATIONALITY
	1 Aus<u>tra</u>lia	Aus<u>tra</u>lian
	2 Bra<u>zil</u>	Bra<u>zil</u>ian
	3 <u>Ca</u>nada	Ca<u>na</u>dian
	4 <u>E</u>gypt	E<u>gyp</u>tian
	5 <u>I</u>taly	I<u>ta</u>lian
	6 <u>Ru</u>ssia	<u>Ru</u>ssian
	7 <u>Ger</u>many	<u>Ger</u>man
	8 <u>Me</u>xico	<u>Me</u>xican
	9 The U<u>ni</u>ted States	A<u>me</u>rican
	10 <u>Chi</u>na	Chi<u>nese</u>
	11 Ja<u>pan</u>	Japa<u>nese</u>
	12 <u>Por</u>tugal	Portu<u>guese</u>
	13 <u>Po</u>land	<u>Po</u>lish
	14 Spain	<u>Spa</u>nish
	15 The <u>UK</u>	<u>Bri</u>tish
	16 France	French

12

Conversations

5 🔘 032 Work with your partner. What nationality are the people? Listen and check.

1 Mo Salah
2 Reese Witherspoon
3 Salma Hayek
4 Marion Cotillard
5 Jürgen Klopp
6 José Mourinho

6 🔘 033 Read and listen to the conversation.

Where are you from?

I'm from the UK. I'm British.

7 What's your nationality? Ask and answer with other students.

8 🔘 034 Read and listen to the blog. Complete the gaps with nationalities. Listen and check.

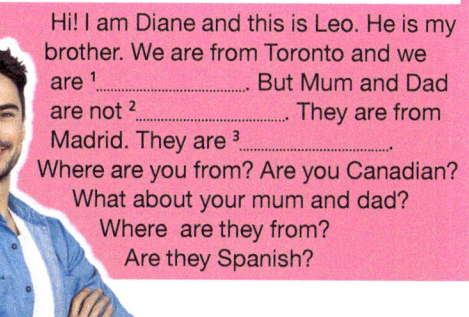

DIANE AND LEO ALMADA

Hi! I am Diane and this is Leo. He is my brother. We are from Toronto and we are ^{1}.................... But Mum and Dad are not ^{2}..................... They are from Madrid. They are ^{3}..................... Where are you from? Are you Canadian? What about your mum and dad? Where are they from? Are they Spanish?

9 Look at the blog again. Underline all the forms of *be*. Then complete the grammar box.

Grammar: *Be*: all forms ▶ PAGE 90

Positive
I ^{1} ......*am*...... from Poland.
He/She/It ^{2}.................... from Italy.
You/We/They ^{3}.................... from Toronto.

Negative
I ^{4} ....*'m not*.... Spanish.
He/She/It ^{5}.................... Canadian.
You/We/They ^{6}.................... Spanish.

Questions
Where ^{7}.................... you/we/they from?
Where ^{8}.................... he/she/it from?
Are you/we/they Canadian?
^{9}.................... he/she/it Spanish?

Short answers
Yes, I **am**. No, I**'m not.**
Yes, you/we/they **are.** No, you/we/they ^{10}....................
Yes, he/she/it **is.** No, he/she/it **isn't.**
Don't use contractions in positive short answers. ~~Yes, I'm.~~

10 Complete the conversation with *am*, *is* or *are*.

Jack: Hello. I'm Jack Mullins.
Ana: Nice to meet you, Jack. I'm Ana and this ^{1}....*is*.... Alex.
Jack: Nice to meet you, too. ^{2}.................... you American?
Alex: No, we aren't. We ^{3}.................... Mexican. ^{4}.................... you American?
Jack: No, I'm not American – I ^{5}....................from Oxford. I'm British. But my mum and dad ^{6}.................... from Nice.
Ana: Nice ^{7}.................... in France – ^{8}.................... I right?
Jack: Yes, you ^{9}.....................
Alex: So they ^{10}.................... French.
Jack: Yes, they ^{11}.....................

11 🔘 035 Listen and check. Practise with a partner.

12 Student A turn to page 98. Student B turn to page 102.

13 Work in pairs. Student A, say a famous person. Student B, say the nationality.

Jose Mourinho. *Portuguese!*

13

2B All about you

- **Grammar:** *Questions*
- **Vocabulary:** *Jobs, Numbers 21–100*
- **Listening:** *Conversations*
- **Pronunciation:** *Intonation in questions*

1 Work with a partner. Match the pictures to the jobs in the box.

> businessman   businesswoman   chef
> doctor   firefighter   nurse   police officer
> teacher   waiter

1 *businessman*   2 ....   3 ....

4 ....   5 ....   6 ....

7 ....   8 ....   9 ....

2 ▶036 Listen, check and repeat.

3 Work with a partner. Ask and answer questions about the people in exercise 1.

> What's her job?   She's a …

4 ▶037 Listen and underline the correct words to complete the conversation.

A: ¹*What's / How's* your name?
B: My name's Chang.
A: ²*What's / How's* your job?
B: I'm a ³*chef / businessman*.
A: How old ⁴*is / are* you?
B: I'm 29. What's your name?

5 Work with a partner. Practise the conversation in exercise 5. Change the job.

6 ▶038 Read and listen to the numbers. Then listen and repeat.

> 21 22 23 24 25 26 27 28 29 30
> 40 50 60 70 80 90 100

7 ▶039 Listen and circle the numbers you hear.

a **19**   **80**   18   **28**
b **6**   16   **60** 66
c **41**   **51**   21   31
d **70**   17   7   **77**
e **62**   **72**   27   **16**
f **95**   **89**   **91** 99

8 Work with a partner. Point to and say the numbers in the photos.

Conversations

9 Ask and answer the questions with your partner.

1 How old are you?

> How old are you?   I'm 36.

2 How old is your mum / your dad / your best friend / your brother / your sister?

> How old is your mum?   My mum is 59.

10 Read the messages. Write the questions in the correct places.

> What's your phone number?   How old are you?
> What's your job?   What's your name?

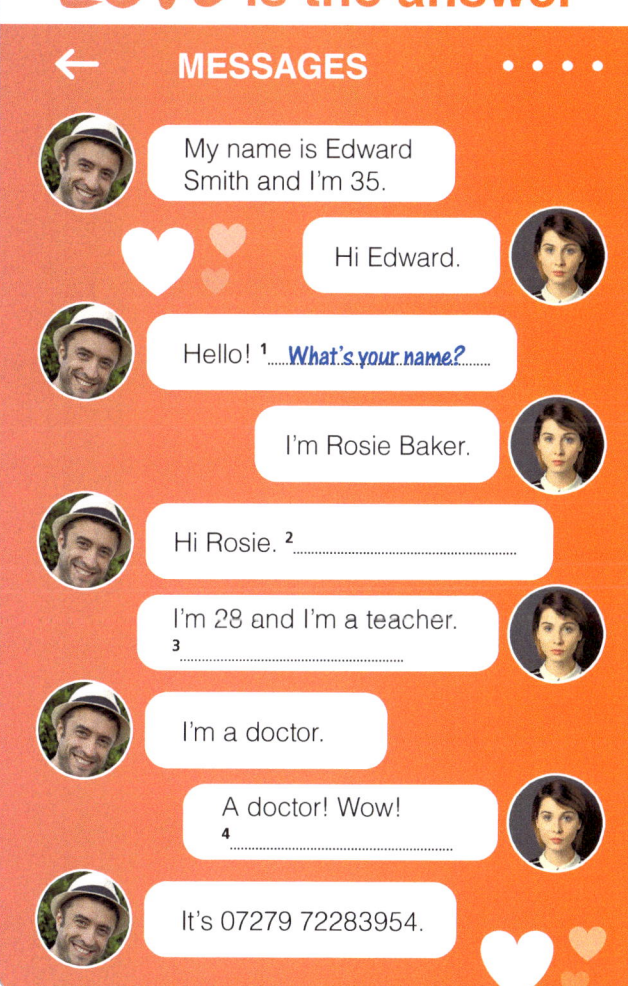

11 ▶ 040 Listen and check. Practise saying the messages with a partner.

12 ▶ 041 Two months later, Rosie calls Edward. Listen and tick what they talk about.

1 a Rosie's job   b Rosie's party
2 a Saturday   b Sunday
3 a a restaurant   b a bar
4 a Edward's friend   b Edward's mum
5 a Edward's house   b Edward's email address

13 ▶ 042 Complete the questions with words from the box. Listen and check.

How (x2)	~~Who~~	What	Where	When

1 '_Who_ is it?'   'It's Rosie.'
2 '............ are you?'   'I'm fine, thanks.'
3 '............ is the party?' 'It's on Saturday at 8 pm.'
4 '............ is it?'   'It's in London.'
5 '............ do you spell it?' 'P-E-P-I-T-O.'
6 '............'s your email address?'
   'It's e_smith@tmail.com.'

Saying email addresses
@ at   . dot   _ underscore

14 Read the grammar box.

Grammar: Questions   ▶ PAGE 91

Question words
What is your name?   **When** is the party?
Who is it?   **Where** is the party?
How are you?   **How old** are you?

Word order
Question word + verb + subject
Where   + is   + the party?

Look:
What 's your email address? = What is
Where 's the party? = Where is

15 Put the words in order to make questions.

1 your / 's / What / name ?   _What's your name?_
2 you / that / How / spell / do ?
3 address / your / What / 's ?
4 you / are / How / old ?
5 's / your best friend / Who ?
6 job / What / your / 's ?
7 birthday / 's / When / your ?
8 email / your / address / 's / What ?

16 ▶ 043 Listen and check. Listen again and repeat.

17 What are your answers to the questions in exercise 15? Ask and answer with other students.

2C Everyday conversations

- Speaking: *Everyday phrases*
- Writing: *A personal profile; Personal information*
- Vocabulary: *Activities*

Speaking

1 ▶ 044 Read and listen to five conversations. Choose the correct words.

A: ¹*Good morning!* / *Good afternoon!*
B: Good morning. Two white coffees, please.
A: Of course.

A: Goodbye! See you ²*next week* / *later*.
B: Bye, Kate.

A: Excuse me. Can I get past?
B: Oh. ³*Thank you* / *I'm sorry*.

A: Here's your card. Have a ⁴*nice day* / *goodbye*.
B: Thanks. And you.

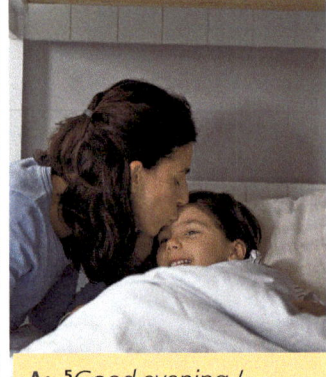

A: ⁵*Good evening* / *Goodnight*. Sleep well.
B: Goodnight, Mum.

2 ▶ 044 Listen again and check.

3 Work with a partner. Practise the conversations.

4 Complete the *Key Language* box with the phrases in the box.

> I'm sorry   Goodnight   Have a nice day
> Good afternoon   See you later

KEY LANGUAGE Everyday phrases

Saying hello
Good morning. ¹.................... . Good evening.
Saying goodbye
² .... See you tomorrow / next week.
³ .... Goodbye / Bye. ⁴ ....
Problems
Excuse me! ⁵ ....

5 Match 1–6 to a–f to make conversations.
1 Good evening.
2 Good morning, Jake! How are you?
3 Bye, Jane.
4 Excuse me!
5 Goodnight.
6 Here's your card. Have a nice day.

a Bye, Luke. See you tomorrow.
b Goodnight. Sleep well.
c Good evening. A table for two, please.
d I'm sorry.
e Thanks. And you.
f Fine, thanks. And you?

6 Match the conversations in exercise 5 to the places.
Restaurant: *Conversation 1*
Street: ....
Shop: ....
Home: ....
Work (x2):   ....

7 ▶ 045 Listen and check your answers.

8 Practise the conversations with a partner.

9 Talk to different students. For each conversation, choose a place from the box. Use the *Key Language*.

> restaurant   street   shop   home   work

Conversations

MAKE NEW FRIENDS
New to BRISTOL? Find new friends here!

Ella
My name's Ella Lewis and I'm 25. I'm Scottish. I'm from Glasgow, but I live in Bristol. I'm a nurse. I'm not married. I like books, music and cooking. My email address is: ellalewis_99@tmail.com

Yuki
My name's Yuki and I'm 29. I'm Japanese. I'm from Tokyo, but I live in Bristol. I'm a businesswoman. I'm not married. I like music, yoga and art. My email address is: yukistar@tmail.com

Jean-Noel
My name's Jean-Noel Legrand and I'm 32. I'm French. I'm from Chambery, but I live in the UK – in Bristol. I'm a chef. I'm not married. I like football, cooking and books. My email address is: jn_legrand@tmail.com

Ilya
I'm Ilya and I'm 29 years old. I'm Russian. I'm from Moscow, but I live in the UK – in Bristol. I'm a businessman. I'm married and my children are two and five years old. I like art, music and football. My email address is: cherni@tmail.com

Writing

1 Read the profiles and answer the questions.
  1 Who is French? ....
  2 Who is a dad? ....
  3 Who is a businesswoman? ....
  4 Who is twenty-five? ....

2 Match the people to their interests.

3 Order the parts of the personal profiles (1–6).
  a I like: ......
  b Job: ......
  c Nationality: ......
  d Name and age: ..1..
  e Email: ......
  f Family: ......

4 Complete the *Key Language* box with the examples in the box.

> I'm a teacher.   running, books and tennis
> jwicks_44@tmail.com
> My name's Rob Jones and I'm 36.
> I'm married to a firefighter.
> I'm Portuguese. I'm from Porto.

KEY LANGUAGE Personal information

Name and age
My name's Ella Lewis and I'm 25. 1 ....
Nationality
I'm Japanese. I'm from Tokyo. 2 ....
Job I'm a chef. 3 ....
Family I'm not married. 4 ....
Likes art, music, and football 5 ....
Email yukistar@tmail.com 6 ....

5 Work with a partner. Match Ella, Jean-Noel, Yuki and Ilya to a new friend. Say why.

> Yuki and Ilya. They're business people and they like art.

6 Write your own personal profile.

> My personal profile
> ....
> ....

7 Give your personal profile to your partner. What is the same? What is different?

> We are both 21.

> You're Spanish, but I'm German.

Video 1: All about me

1 Ask and answer the questions with a partner.
   1 What's your name?
   2 How do you spell it?
   3 Where are you from?
   4 How old are you?
   5 What's your job?

2 ▶ Watch the first question on the video and write the name of each person in the profiles. Watch the second question and check the spelling.

My name is ....
I am from ....
I am .... years old.
I am a ....

My name is ....
I am from ....
I am .... years old.
I am a ....

My name is ....
I am from ....
I am .... years old.
I am a ....

My name is ....
I am from ....
I am .... years old.
I am a ....

My name is ....
I am from ....
I am .... years old.
I am a ....

3 Work with a partner. Match the places you think each person is from to a profile.

London

Lima, Peru

France

Sydney, Australia

Sevilla, Spain

4 Watch the next question on the video and check where each person is from. Write the places in the profiles.

5 Work with a partner. How old do you think each person is?

> I think Reice is about 20 years old.

> I think Pepa is about 28 years old.

6 Watch the video again and check. Add the answers to their profile.

7 Watch the last question and add jobs to the profiles.

8 Work with new partner. Ask and answer the questions. Write a profile of your partner.

My name is ....
I'm from ....
I'm .... years old.
I'm a ....

Review

LESSON 1A	Introduce yourself to someone else.
LESSON 1A	Say the days of the week out loud.
LESSON 1B	Write the names of 6 countries in English.
LESSON 1B	Ask someone where they are from.
LESSON 1C	Spell the name of someone you know well.
LESSON 1C	Say your phone number out loud in English.
LESSON 2A	Write a nationality for each of these letters: *a, b, c, e, f, m, r, s*
LESSON 2A	Write 3 sentences about famous people. Use *is* and *are* in the sentences.
LESSON 2B	Name 5 jobs in English.
LESSON 2B	Start at 100 and count backwards in English. How far can you get before you make a mistake?
LESSON 2C	Write a response to these expressions. *How are you? Have a good evening. Good night.*
LESSON 2C	Write a profile of yourself. Include: name, age, nationality, job, family, things you like.

19

3 Things

> Vocabulary: *My things*
> Grammar: *Singular and plural nouns*
> Pronunciation: *Plurals*

3A My things

1 Match the pictures to the words in the box.

| bag brushes bank card desks laptop keys |
| notebook pen pencils purses umbrella |
| wallet watches |

2 ▶049 Listen, check and repeat.

3 Which words in exercise 1 are singular, and which are plural?

4 ▶050 Listen to the pronunciation of the plural nouns. Listen again and repeat.

/s/	/z/	/ɪz/
desks	pencils	watches

5 ▶051 Add the words to the table in exercise 4. Listen and check. Listen again and repeat.

purses   keys   wallets

6 Complete the grammar box.

a   an   -es   some

Grammar: Singular and plural nouns; *a / an* ▶PAGE 91

Singular nouns

We use *a* or *an* + singular noun.

We use ¹................... + word beginning with a consonant: **a** brush

We use ²...................+ word beginning with a vowel: **an** umbrella

Plural nouns

We use a number or ³................... + plural nouns: two pens, some desks

Spelling rules

+ -s: two keys, three pencils

+ ⁴................... : two watches, some brushes

We add -es to words ending in *ch*, *sh*, *ss* and *x*.

20

7 〔052〕 Match the pictures to the words in the box. Listen and check.

two buses   two cities   an email   some houses
a pizza   three phones   a taxi   some tickets

8 〔053〕 Read and listen.

1
What's this?
I don't know. I think it's a key
Yes, you're right.

2
What's this?
I don't know. I think they're buses.
I'm not sure.

9 Look at the photos. What are the things? Work with a partner.

I think it's a / an...   *I think they're...*

10 〔054〕 Listen and match the people to the things.

keys
pen
1 Sam
purse
2 Eva
wallet
umbrella

11 Write the names of three things in your bag or pocket. Then tell your partner.

In my bag I have ....

12 What other things do you have in your bag? Ask your teacher.

How do you say... in English?   *How do you spell that?*

3B Shopping

> **Grammar:** *This, that, these, those*
> **Vocabulary:** *Clothes and colours*
> **Listening:** *Shopping*

1 Match the pictures to the words in the box.

> coat   dress   hat   jacket   jeans   shirt   shoes
> skirt   trousers   T-shirt

2 ▶ 055 Listen and check. Then listen and repeat.

3 Which clothes are plural?

4 Match the words in the box to the colours.

> black   blue   brown   green   grey   orange
> pink   red   white   yellow

5 Write the colours of the clothes in exercise 1.

a green hat
some yellow trousers

6 ▶ 056 Listen to the people in a clothes shop. Complete the sentences.
1 Ooh, look! That .... dress is nice! How much is it?
2 I like those red .... But they're £200!
3 I like this .... hat. It's very nice! It's only £2!
4 Those .... are lovely! How much are they?
5 Can I have one of those ....? The grey one.
6 How much are these ....?

7 Circle *this*, *that*, *these* and *those* in exercise 6.

8 Look at the pictures and complete the grammar box.

> **Grammar:** *This, that, these* and *those*   ▶ PAGE 91
>
> We use **this** / ¹ .... for things near us.
> We use **that** / ² .... for things that aren't near us.
> We use ³ .... and .... for singular nouns.
> We use ⁴ .... and .... for plural nouns.
>
> Note: Some things are always plural e.g. *trousers*, *glasses*, *jeans*.

this T-shirt

these dresses

that jacket

those shoes

Things

9 🔊057 Complete the sentences with *this*, *that*, *these* and *those*. Listen and check.

1 .... red T-shirt isn't very nice!

2 Are .... your clothes?

3 Is .... your phone over there?

4 .... are my children.

5 How much are .... black hats?

6 How much is .... blue shirt?

10 Student A look at the picture below. Student B turn to page 103.
1 Look at the prices on your picture.
2 Ask Student B questions to find the missing prices.
3 Add the missing prices to your picture.

How much is this …?   How much is that …?
How much are these …?   How much are those …?

23

3C Out and about

▶ Speaking: In a café; Prices
▶ Writing: A form; Capital letters

Speaking

1 Work with a partner. Where is the money from? How much is there?

2 ▶058 Listen and check

3 Match the prices and the words.
1 $4.99   c a fifty cents
2 75p   b one pound and thirty pence
3 $0.50   c four dollars ninety-nine cents
4 £5.85   d seventy five pence
5 €12.98   e two dollars eighty cents
6 €3.45   f twelve euros and ninety-eight cents
7 $2.80   g five pounds eighty-five
8 £1.30   h three euros and forty-five cents

4 ▶059 Listen, check and repeat.

5 ▶060 Listen to three conversations. Choose the correct prices.

		a	b
1	black coffee	£1.85	£1.95
2	cheese sandwich	$4.15	$4.50
3	salad	€4.49	€9.49

6 Work with a partner. Ask the prices on the menu below.

How much is the soup? 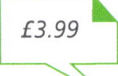   *£3.99*

7 ▶061 Listen to Tim in a café. Tick the things on the menu that he orders.

8 Complete the Key Language box with the words in the box.

| else | have | fine | is | please |

KEY LANGUAGE In a café

Can I ¹ .... a chicken wrap, please?
Anything ² ....?
A black coffee, ³ ....
How much ⁴ .... it?
Yes, that's ⁵ .... Thank you.

9 ▶061 Listen again and check. Which things in the Key Language box does Tim say?

10 ▶062 Put the conversation in the correct order. Listen and check.

a How much is it?   ☐
b Anything else?   ☐
c Who's next?   1
d There you go.   ☐
e Can I have a cheese sandwich, please? ☐
f £7.85. Here's the machine. ☐
g And a cola, please.   ☐
h Yes, that's fine. Thank you. ☐

YOUR TURN

11 Practise the conversation in exercise 10.
Student A: you are the customer. Change the food you order.
Student B: you are the waiter. Change the prices.

12 Swap roles and practise again.

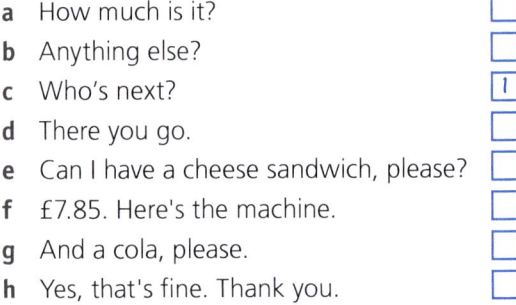

MENU

FOOD
Soup   £3.99
Burger   £6.99
Chicken wrap   £3.80
Ice cream   £3.49

DRINK
Mineral water £1.90
Orange juice   £2.10
Beer   £4.00
Coffee / tea   £1.95

Things

Writing

1 Look at the form. Match each part to a question.

1 What's your address?
2 What's your postcode?
3 Are you married?
4 How old are you?
5 What's your phone number?
6 What's your email?
7 What's your name?

2 Complete the form for you.

FIT GYM

Personal details
A Title Mr   Ms   Mrs
  First name
  Surname
B Age
C Married   Single
  Divorced/Separated
D Address
E Postcode
F Email
G Phone number

3 Read the *Key Language* box. Check your capital letters in the form.

KEY LANGUAGE Capital letters

We use capital letters for:
Names: Paul Simpson
Addresses: 55 Kings Road
Towns, cities and countries: Manchester, London, France

4 Correct the mistakes in the sentences.
 1 My name is harry Roberts.
 2 I live at 129 green lane.
 3 I'm from london.
 4 My name is marie Clay. I am from new York.
 5 I'm from scotland. I live in Glasgow.
 6 My address is 204 lime street.

YOUR TURN

5 Work with a partner. Ask the questions in exercise 1 to complete the form for your partner. Remember to use capital letters

CENTRAL HOTEL

PERSONAL DETAILS

First name
Surname
Title   Mr   Ms   Mrs
Age
Married   Single   Divorced/Separated
Address
Postcode
Email
Phone number

25

4 People and places

> - **Vocabulary:** *Family; Adjectives for people*
> - **Reading:** *A blog*
> - **Pronunciation:** *'s*
> - **Grammar:** *Possessives*

4A Family and friends

1 Look at the photo. Match the words in the box to the people.

> boy   girl   man   woman

1 Tom is a ………………….
2 Ben is a ………………….
3 Ivy is a ………………….
4 Eva is a ………………….

2 ▶ 065 Listen and check. Listen again and repeat.

3 ▶ 066 Read and listen to Lisa and Dan. Answer the questions. Write the names.
1 Who is a firefighter? ……Tom……
2 Who is five years old? ………………….
3 Who is a businessman? ………………….
4 Who is 36? ………………….
5 Who is a teacher? ………………….

4 Work with a partner. Look at the pictures in the table. Complete the table with the underlined family words in the text.

woman	¹wife	²mother, ³…………
man	⁴…………	⁵father, ⁶…………
		mum + dad = ⁷…………
boy		⁸son, ⁹…………
girl		¹⁰…………, ¹¹sister

5 ▶ 067 Listen and check. Listen again and repeat.

BEST friends

LISA

My name's Lisa, I'm 36 and my best friend is Eva. She's 33 and she's a businesswoman. Here's a photo of Eva and her family on holiday. The man in the photo is Eva's <u>husband</u>, Tom. He's a firefighter. They have two children, a boy and a girl. **Their** <u>son</u> is five and his name is Ben. Their <u>daughter</u> is the baby – **her** name is Ivy. Here's a photo of Eva and her family on holiday. So who is **your** best friend?

DAN

My name's Dan. I'm 25 and I'm a businessman. My best friend is my <u>brother</u> – **our** <u>mum</u> and <u>dad</u> are very happy about that! My brother's name is Joe and he's a teacher. The woman in the blue jacket is **his** wife, Emma. She is also a teacher. Emma's <u>sister</u>, Jenny, is my girlfriend! My <u>parents</u> are also friends with Emma and Jenny's parents! Here's a photo of me with Jenny, Emma and Joe.

6 Choose the correct words to complete sentences about Eva's family.
1 Tom is Eva's *dad* / *husband*.
2 Ivy is Eva's *daughter* / *wife*.
3 Ben is Ivy's *husband* / *brother*.
4 Eva is Ben's *mum* / *sister*.
5 Tom and Eva are Ivy's *parents* / *children*.
6 Tom is Ben and Ivy's *son* / *father*.

7 Look at the words in bold below. Read the grammar box and find more examples of possessives in the text about Lisa and Dan.

Here's a photo of Eva and **her** family.
The man in the photo is **Eva's** husband, Tom.

Grammar: *Possessives* ▶ PAGE 91

We can use possessive adjectives or possessive 's to talk about possession.

Possessive adjectives

my, your, his, her, its, our, their

Possessive 's

*Emma is **his** wife.* > *Emma is Joe's wife.*
*Tom is **her** husband.* > *Tom is Eva's husband.*

Is = 's

We also use 's to say *is*: *My name's Dan.* (*My name is Dan.*)
He's a teacher. (*He is a teacher.*)

8 Complete the table with words and examples from the text about Lisa and Dan.

		Possessive adjective	Example
1	I	my	My name is Lisa.
2	you		
3	he		
4	she		
5	we		
6	they		

9 Work with a partner. Complete the sentences with the correct possessive adjectives.
  1 'Is Katie ……*your*…… daughter?' 'Yes, she is.'
  2 'Are your parents Portuguese?' 'No, ……………… parents are Brazilian.'
  3 My brother is 15. ……………… name is Max.
  4 'Who are your parents?' '……………… names are Claire and Paul.'
  5 This is my sister. ……………… name is Molly. ……………… mum and dad are doctors.

10 Read the grammar box again. Look at 's in the sentences. Write (P) for possessive 's or (I) for *is*.
  1 My name**'s** Marco. ……*I*……
  2 Her brother**'s** wife is Mexican. ………
  3 My dad**'s** a police officer. ………
  4 My wife**'s** name is Tara. ………
  5 What**'s** your name? ………
  6 Here**'s** a photo of me. ………

11 068 Listen to the sentences in exercise 10. What sound is 's? Is it /s/ or /z/? Practise saying the sentences.

12 069 Work with a partner. Look at the family tree and listen to the sentences. Then take turns to make more sentences.

Vikram   Prisha
Dev   Mina

Vikram is Prisha's husband.
Dev is Vikram's son.

13 070 Listen to Prisha and Dev talking about their family. How old is each person?
  1 Prisha ………………   3 Dev ………………
  2 Vikram ………………   4 Mina ………………

14 070 Listen again and complete the sentences with the words in the box.

| young   old   clever x 2   lazy   funny |

  1 My husband Vikram is very ……*clever*…… He's a teacher.
  2 You're ……………… too, Mum. You're a doctor!
  3 But you and Dad are ……………… .
  4 You're eight – so you're ………………!
  5 Mina is five – she's young, and she's ……………… .
  6 But Dad says I'm ……………… .

15 Draw your family tree.

16 Show a partner your family tree. Take turns to ask and answer about your family.

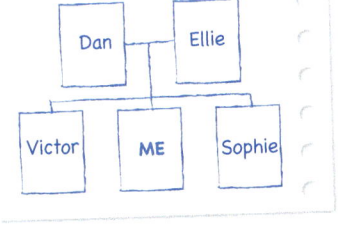

Who's Victor?
Victor's my brother. He's 22 – he's young … and he's lazy!

4B My home and my things

- **Grammar:** Adjectives; have/has
- **Vocabulary:** Adjectives for places and things
- **Reading:** My brother and sister
- **Listening:** What's new?

1 ▶ 071 Read and listen to Kelly talking about her brother and sister. Write Jack or Rosie for each photo.

1 ....

2 ....

3 ....

4 ....

Jack and Rosie

Jack is my brother. He's 31 and he's a banker. He likes **expensive** things – he has a **new** car and he has a **beautiful** house. His house is **big** – it has ten bedrooms and it's an **old** house – it's 200 years old!

My sister's name is **Rosie**. She's 21 and she's a student. She has a **small** car because it's **cheap**. Her car is also **old** but she loves it. She has a nice house but it's **ugly** – it's orange and black!

2 Read the text again. Match the adjectives in bold in the text to the pictures.

1

2

5

6

3

4

7

8

3 ▶ 072 Listen, check and repeat.

4 Read the grammar box. Write the examples in the box in the correct place.

> She has a small car.   Her car is old.
> The cars are expensive.

Grammar: Adjectives ▶ PAGE 92

The adjective goes AFTER the verb.

*His house **is big**.*

1 ....

The adjective goes BEFORE the noun.

*He has a **new car**.*

2 ....

Adjectives are the same for both the singular AND the plural.

*The houses **are new**.*

3 ....

5 Put the words in the correct order to make sentences.

1 parents / old / are / My *My parents are old.*
2 beautiful / It's / dress / a ....
3 The / pens / cheap / are ....
4 young / a / Roger / has / wife
....
5 is / small / Her / bag ....
6 watches / They / are / expensive
....
7 is / My / house / big / doctor's
....
8 My / new / phone / is ....

6 ▶ 073 Listen, check and repeat.

People and places

7 Work with a partner. Talk about these things. Use adjectives from exercise 2.

> my bag   my house   my car   my city   my pen
> my bag   my laptop   my phone

My bag is small and expensive.

Really? My bag is big and old.

8 ▶074 Listen to Kelly. Underline the correct words.
1 Kelly's apartment is in *Oxford / London*.
2 Laura is a *doctor / businesswoman*.
3 Rosie has a new *apartment / car*.
4 *Kelly's parents / Jack and Rosie* have a house by the sea.
5 Lucky is *small and beautiful / big and brown*.

9 ▶074 Listen again and complete the sentences with *have*, *don't have*, *has* or *doesn't have*.
1 I .... a new apartment in Oxford.
2 I .... two bedrooms.
3 I .... a garden, but there's a balcony.
4 And what about Jack? Does he .... some news?
5 Jack .... a girlfriend!
6 She .... a job in London.
7 Rosie .... a job so she .... money!
8 She .... a boyfriend, but she is fine about that.
9 Our parents .... a new house by the sea.
10 And they .... a new dog.

10 Complete the grammar box.

Grammar: have/has   ▶PAGE 92

Have is an irregular verb. We use it to talk about possession.

Positive
I/you/we/they ¹............... a new car.
He/she/it ²............... a new car.

Negative
I ³............... **have** a garden.
She ⁴............... **have** a boyfriend.

Questions
⁵............... you **have** a new car?
Yes, I **do**. / No, I **don't**.
⁶............... he/she **have** a new car?
Yes, he **does**. / No, he **doesn't**.

11 Choose the correct words to complete the sentences.
1 My parents *has / have* an old car.
2 Does your sister *has / have* a boyfriend?
3 We *have / has* an expensive car.
4 Her brother *have / has* an ugly dog.
5 *Have you / Do you have* a house by the sea?
6 I *has / have* a clever son.
7 *Do / Does* you have a beautiful house?
8 I *not have / don't have* a watch.

12 ▶075 Listen, check and repeat.

13 Stand up and talk to other students. Ask questions and complete the chart.

Find someone who has ...	NAME	More information
a clever brother		
an ugly car		
an expensive watch		
an old dog		
a house by the sea		
a beautiful friend		
a small car		
a cheap phone		
a lazy sister		
a new house		

29

4C A night out

▶ **Speaking:** *Talking about time*
▶ **Writing:** *Someone in my family; Adverbs*

Speaking

1 **076** Listen and repeat the times.

1 It's nine o'clock. 2 It's five past nine.

3 It's ten past nine. 4 It's a quarter past nine.

5 It's twenty past nine. 6 It's twenty-five past nine.

7 It's half past nine. 8 It's twenty-five to ten.

9 It's twenty to ten. 10 It's a quarter to ten.

11 It's ten to ten. 12 It's five to ten.

2 Work with a partner. Take turns to say the times on the clocks in exercise 1.

3 **077** Listen and match the conversations to the places.

   A bus stop = conversation ....
   B restaurant = conversation ....
   C office = conversation ....

4 **077** Complete the conversations with the words in the box. Then listen again and check.

> late past twenty-five it seven sorry
> OK time next so

Conversation 1
L: What time is ¹.................., Jane?
J: It's ².................. o'clock.
L: OK. Thanks. It's time to go home!

Conversation 2
L: Er. Excuse me. What's the ³..................?
M: It's half ⁴.................. seven.
L: Oh no! I'm ⁵.................. for my dinner date. What time is the ⁶.................. bus to the city centre?
M: The next bus is at ten to eight.

Conversation 3
L: Oh, hi, Anna. ⁷.................. I'm late!
A: Hi, Luke Yes – you're ⁸.................. minutes late!
L: I'm ⁹.................. sorry, Anna.
A: That's ¹⁰.................. Let's order some drinks.

5 Work with a partner. Practise the conversations in exercise 4.

6 Complete the *Key Language* box with phrases from the box.

> That's OK. Sorry I'm late. What time is it?
> The next bus is at ten to eight.

KEY LANGUAGE Talking about the time

Asking about the time
¹.................. What's the time?
What time is the next bus/train to … ?
Giving the time/information
It's seven o'clock/half past seven. ².................
Problems
³.................. I'm so sorry. ⁴..................

YOUR TURN

7 Student A turn to page 99. Student B turn to page 103.

30

People and places

Writing

1 Think about three people in your family and choose an adjective for each one. Tell your partner and give more information.

My brother is clever. He's a doctor.

2 Read about Katie. Answer the questions.
  1 Where is she at 10 am every day?
  2 Does she have a house or an apartment?
  3 What's her job?
  4 What is her first book about?
  5 Does she have a boyfriend?
  6 Who is Alf?

My lazy sister, Katie

My sister, Katie is very lazy. She is still in bed at 10 am every day. She loves sleeping and she is always late! She has an apartment in Birmingham. Her apartment is quite new and it's very expensive. It's £900 per month! She's a writer and her book is really good – it's about a nurse in the 1950s. Does she have a boyfriend? No – not now, but she has a beautiful cat. The cat's name is Alf and he is also very lazy!

10 o'clock in the morning

2 o'clock in the afternoon

11 o'clock at night

3 Look at the adverbs in the box. Find and underline them in the text about Katie.

quite   now   very   still   really   also

4 Read the Key Language box. Write the headings in the correct place.

For time, or to say when   To add information
To say how much

KEY LANGUAGE Common adverbs

1	2	3 ....
quite (small)	now	also
very (big)	still	
really (big)		

5 Complete the conversation with adverbs from the Key Language box.

My grandad, Mick

A: What's your grandad's name?
B: His name is Mick and he is ¹ _really_ old – he's 90!
A: Does he have a house or an apartment?
B: His home town is York and he ² .... lives there, after 90 years! He has a small house there. I ³ .... live in York with my wife.
A: Does he have a dog?
B: No, not ⁴ ...., but he has a cat.
A: Does he have a big car?
B: He has a Skoda Octavia – it's ⁵ .... big, but not really big.

6 Write 80–100 words about a person in your family. Use adverbs and adjectives.

7 Swap texts with a partner. Read your partner's text. How many adjectives and adverbs are there?

Video 2: Family tree

2: Family tree

1 Work with a partner. Discuss the questions.
  1 What's your mother's name?
  2 What's your father's name?
  3 How old are they?

2 Look at the family tree. Complete the sentences.

The Garcia Family

 +

This is Diego Garcia. He's Spanish. He is 49 years old.

This is Ana Martinho. She's Portuguese. She's 48 years old.

This is Pablo. He's 22 years old.

This is Gabriela. She's 19 years old.

1 Diego is Ana's ……husband…….
2 Ana is Diego's ………………….
3 Diego is Pablo's and Gabriela's ………………….
4 Ana is Pablo's and Gabriela's ………………….
5 Pablo's ……………… is Gabriela.
6 Gabriela's ……………… is Pablo.
7 Gabriela is the ……………… of Ana and Diego.
8 Pablo is the ……………… of Ana and Diego.
9 Ana and Diego are the ……………… of Pablo and Gabriela.

3 Write the countries they are from.
  1 Diego is from ……………….
  2 Ana is from ……………….

4 Write their ages in words.
  1 Diego is ……………… years old.
  2 Ana is ……………… years old.
  3 Pablo is ……………… years old.
  4 Gabriela is ……………… years old.

5 ▶ Watch the video. Tick ✓ the number of people that Joe talks about.

   9   10   11   12

6 ▶ Watch the video again. Complete the sentences about Joe's Family.
1 Joe's .... is called Hannah.
2 Joe's .... is called Michael.
3 Joe's ...., Lotte and Jan, are from the Netherlands.
4 His dad's parents are from Glasgow, in ....
5 Joe's uncle, his dad's ...., is in Chicago, in America.
6 Paul's .... is called Stacy.
7 Paul and Stacy have two children. George is .... years old and Megan is .... years old.

7 Write the names and ages of these people in your family. Tell a partner about the people.
1 Your brothers and sisters ....
2 Your aunts and uncles ....

My sister's name is Lucia. She's twenty-eight years old.

My uncle's name is Marco. He's sixty-three years old.

Review

LESSON 3A	Name 3 things in your pocket or bag.
LESSON 3A	Write the plural of these nouns: *key*, *pencil*, *watch*, *brush*.
LESSON 3B	Name 5 kinds of clothes.
LESSON 3B	Is *this* or *that* for things near you? Is *this* or *those* for plural nouns? Is *that* or *these* for plural nouns?
LESSON 3C	Write three useful phrases for a café.
LESSON 3C	Write these sentences with the correct capital letters. *I'm sam bailey from edinburgh.*
LESSON 4A	Write 3 sentences about your family. Use *my*, *his* and *her*.
LESSON 4A	Use adjectives to write 3 sentences about your family.
LESSON 4B	Write a sentence with an adjective *after* a verb. Write a sentence with an adjective before a noun.
LESSON 4B	What is the opposite of these adjectives? *big*, *new*, *expensive*, *old*
LESSON 4C	Write the time now.
LESSON 4C	Write 3 adverbs *to say how much*.

33

5 My life

▶ **Vocabulary:** Sport and free time
▶ **Grammar:** Present Simple positive and negative: I/you/we/they
▶ **Listening:** Activities

I play computer games every evening, and I go to the cinema. I don't do exercise.

Hana

I do exercise every day. I play tennis, I play football and I go running.

Mark

5A Activities

1 ▶079 Read and listen to Hana and Mark. Which person is like you?

2 Match the pictures to the words in the box.

| beach   board games   cinema   computer games
| cycling   exercise   basketball   running   shopping
| swimming   tennis   drama |

3 ▶080 Listen and check.

My life

4 ▶081 Listen to six people. Write the correct activity for each person.

1 .... 4 ....
2 .... 5 ....
3 .... 6 ....

5 ▶081 Look at the underlined verbs in exercise 1. Listen again. Complete the sentences with *do*, *play* or *go*.

1 We .... to the beach.
2 I .... tennis.
3 They .... exercise.
4 I .... computer games.
5 They .... running.
6 I .... swimming.

6 Put the activities in exercises 2–5 in the correct column.

play	go	do
board games	swimming	exercise

7 ▶082 Listen and check your answers. Then listen and repeat.

8 ▶083 Complete the profiles with the words in the box. Listen and check.

do (x2)   don't do   don't go   go (x4)   play

Nori
I like sport. I ¹.................................. a lot of exercise. I ².................................. basketball and tennis and I ³.................................. running once a week. My friends go cycling a lot. They go three times a week. I ⁴.................................. cycling every Sunday afternoon with them.

Amy
I like films. I ⁵.................................. to the cinema a lot with my friends. In the summer, I also ⁶.................................. to the beach a lot, but I ⁷.................................. swimming in the sea. I don't like swimming! I ⁸.................................. a lot of exercise, but I ⁹.................................. yoga once a week.

9 Read the grammar box. Find more examples of Present Simple verbs in exercise 8.

Grammar: Present Simple positive and negative: *I, you, we, they* ▶ PAGE 92

Positive

I/you/we/they **play** computer games every day.

Negative

I/you/we/they **don't play** board games.

We use the Present Simple for things we usually do: *I go running every day. We don't go cycling every weekend.*

10 Put the words in the correct order.

1 swimming / My parents / go / don't
2 play / board games / My brothers
3 I / go to the / with my friends / beach
4 do / You / drama
5 play / basketball / My sisters
6 go to the / cinema / We

11 Write one positive sentence and one negative sentence with the verb in bold.

do   We ¹ *don't do* very much exercise but we ² *do* drama once a week.

go   They ³.................................. running very often but they ⁴.................................. cycling three times a week.

play   I ⁵.................................. board games with my children but I ⁶.................................. computer games. My children play computer games a lot!

12 Write sentences about you.

1 I play ....
2 I don't play ....
3 I do ....
4 I don't do ....
5 I go ....
6 I don't go ....

13 Work with a partner. Talk about your activities. Then write sentences about both of you.

We play tennis and we go running.

14 In groups of four, share your sentences from exercise 13. Tell the class about the other pair.

> Sam and Leila play tennis and they go running.

35

5B Chatting

- **Grammar:** Present Simple questions: I/you/we/they
- **Vocabulary:** Common verbs and nouns together
- **Listening:** Conversations

1 ▶ 084 Read and listen. Match the conversations to the pictures.

1
A: Do you want coffee or tea?
B: Coffee, please.

2
A: Do you like that book?
B: Yes, I do. I love her books. She's my favourite writer.

3
A: Do you live in Birmingham?
B: No, I don't. I live in Manchester with my husband and two children. Do you have children?
A: No, I don't. How old are your children?
B: I have a boy and a girl. Sophie is six and Nate is four. Look. Here are some photos.

2 Read the conversations again. Complete the grammar box with *do* and *don't*.

Grammar: Present Simple questions:
I, you, we, they ▶ PAGE 92

Questions
Do you *like* that book?
¹................... they **have** children?
Do we **need** a new car?

Short answers
Yes, I/you/we/they ²................... .
No, I/you/we/they ³................... .

3 Complete the conversations with *do* and *don't*.

A
¹................... you have a brother or sister?
Yes, I ²................... . I have one brother.

B
³................... you want a coffee?
No, I thanks. I ⁴................... drink coffee.

C
⁵................... you speak German?
No, I ⁶................... . I only speak English.

D
⁷................... you have an umbrella? It's raining.
Yes, I ⁸................... . Here you go.

4 ▶ 085 Listen and check. Practise the conversations in pairs.

A

B

C

My life

5 086 Complete the phrases with the verbs in the box. Listen and check.

drink   eat   have   listen   live   read   speak   want   watch

1 .... in a flat

2 .... coffee

3 .... TV

4 .... a new car

5 .... a cat

6 .... a book

7 .... to music

8 .... breakfast

9 .... English

6 Write five sentences about you. Use the verbs and nouns in exercise 5. Compare with a partner
I live in a flat. I don't have a cat.

7 Complete the questions with verbs from exercise 5.
1 *Do you read* newspapers online?
2 .... Netflix?
3 .... a dog?
4 .... Chinese food?
5 .... in a house?
6 .... to the radio?
7 .... French?
8 .... breakfast every morning?
9 .... cola?

8 Work with a partner. Ask and answer the questions.

9 Write six more questions starting with *Do you …?*

10 Ask and answer your questions with your partner. Add more information.

Do you drink tea?

No, I don't. I drink coffee.

Do you listen to hip hop?

Yes, I do. I like hip hop.

37

5C Talking about yourself

> • **Speaking:** Making small talk; Wh- questions
> • **Vocabulary:** Question words
> • **Writing:** A blog; And/because

Speaking

1  **087** Listen to four conversations. Match the conversations to the pictures.

A — jobs
B — family

C — hobbies
D — home

2 Complete the questions with words from the box.

| Do (x2)   What   When   Where |
| Which   Who (x2) |

1 .... do you live?
2 .... do you work for?
3 .... do you do?
4 .... you play for a team?
5 .... do you play? At the weekend?
6 .... team is your favourite?
7 .... you have a big family?
8 .... do you spend time with at the weekend?

3 **087** Listen again and check.

4 Complete the *Key Language* box with the words in the box.

> what   when   where   who   which

KEY LANGUAGE *Wh-* questions

We use ¹................ for people.
We use ²................ for things and facts.
We use ³................ for places.
We use ⁴................ for times.
We use ⁵................ for people and things when there is a limited choice.

5 Put the words in the correct order.
1 do / where / work / you ?
2 do / in your free time / what / you / do ?
3 do / exercise / you / when / do ?
4 your / food / favourite / What's ?
5 when / you / do / get up ?
6 favourite / who / your / is / singer ?
7 favourite / is / what / your / TV programme ?
8 really like / which / city / do / you ?

6 Work in pairs. Ask and answer the questions in exercise 5.

YOUR TURN

7 Write five questions to ask other students.
1 What ....?
2 When ....?
3 Where ....?
4 Who ....?
5 Which ....?

8 Answer your own questions in exercise 7.

9 Move around the class and ask your questions to other students. Who gives the same answers as you?

> *What's your favourite city?*
>
> *It's Paris. I really like Paris!*

My life

Writing

1 Read the blog. Complete it with the words in the box.

> don't see   eat   finish   go (x3)   live (x2)
> play (x2)   read   start   watch   work

My BUSY week

I ¹............... in Sydney, in Australia. I ²............... in a flat with my girlfriend. We ³............... each other much in the week because we both work a lot. I ⁴............... in an office. I ⁵............... work at eight in the morning and I ⁶............... work at seven in the evening. In the evenings we ⁷............... dinner together and we ⁸............... Netflix before we go to bed.

The weekends are fun. I ⁹............... football on Saturday mornings with my friends. In the afternoon I ¹⁰............... tennis with my girlfriend or we ¹¹............... for a walk. In the evening we ¹²............... out for dinner or we ¹³............... to the cinema. On Sundays we are very lazy. We stay in bed in the morning, then we ¹⁴............... the newspapers. We often visit my girlfriend's parents in the afternoon. We don't see my parents very often because they live in a different city.

2 Write five sentences about activities you do every week.

3 Find examples of *and* and *because* in the blog. Then complete the *Key Language* box with *and* and *because*.

> **KEY LANGUAGE** *and/because*
>
> We use ¹............... to join ideas. *We have dinner together **and** we watch Netflix.*
>
> We use ²............... to give a reason. *We don't see each other much **because** we both work long hours.*

4 Complete the sentences with *and* or *because*.
 1 I drive to work .... I work in a different city.
 2 I live with my parents .... my sister.
 3 I don't do much exercise .... I don't have time.
 4 On Fridays, I see my friends .... we go to the cinema.
 5 I'm a waiter .... I work in the city centre.
 6 I'm really tired in the evenings .... I start work at seven in the morning.
 7 I love my flat .... it is near lots of shops, cafés, bars .... restaurants.
 8 I have a dog .... a cat.

YOUR TURN

5 Write a blog about your weekdays and your weekend. Use *and* to join ideas and *because* to give reasons.

6 Work in groups. Read all the blogs. Can you guess the people?

39

6 Routines

- **Vocabulary:** Verbs for daily routines
- **Grammar:** Adverbs of frequency
- **Pronunciation:** /s/ and /z/, Missing sounds
- **Reading:** Mark's Mondays

6A My routine

1 Work with a partner. Discuss the questions.
1. Do you go to bed early or late? Why?
2. Which days of the week do you like? Why?

> I go to bed late because I watch TV in the evenings.

> I like Thursdays because I play football after work.

2 ▶089 Read and listen to Mark. When does his day start and end?

Mark's Mondays

I always <u>get up</u> at 7:00 on work days.

Then I <u>have a shower</u> and <u>get dressed</u>.

I have breakfast at 7:30. I usually have cornflakes.

I <u>leave home</u> at 8:00. I usually <u>cycle to work</u>, or I sometimes <u>take the bus</u>.

I buy coffee at work. I never drink coffee at home. I usually <u>leave work</u> at 6:00.

I <u>get home</u> at 7:00 and I <u>have dinner</u> at 7:30. I often watch TV in the evening.   I always <u>go to bed</u> at 11:30.

3 Look at the underlined phrases in the text. Then cover the text and complete the phrases with the verbs in the box.

| cycle | get | go | have | leave | take |

1. **have** .... a shower / dinner
2. .... up / dressed / home
3. .... home / work
4. .... to work
5. .... the bus
6. .... to bed

4 Work with a partner. Ask and answer the questions about your Mondays.

On Mondays, what time do you … ?

get up / have a shower / leave home / leave work or school / get home / have dinner / go to bed

> On Mondays, what time do you get up?

> I get up at half past six.

40

Routines

5 Look at the adverbs in the box. Find them in Mark's text.

> always   usually   often   sometimes   never

6 Read the grammar box. Complete it with the adverbs from exercise 5.

Grammar: Adverbs of frequency   ▶ PAGE 93

Adverbs of frequency give more information about routines.

I get up at nine o'clock. > *I **usually** get up at 9 o'clock.*

Adverbs of frequency come <u>after</u> the subject and <u>before</u> the verb.

*I **always** go to bed at 10 o'clock.*

We use adverbs of frequency to say how often we do something.

0%	30%	60%	85%	100%
1 _never_	2 _____	3 _often_	4 _____	5 _____

7 🔊 090 Listen and check. Answer the questions. Then listen again and repeat.
1. Do *always* and *sometimes* end with an /s/ or a /z/ sound?
2. Which letter do you NOT hear in *often*?
3. Which letter do you NOT hear in *usually*?

8 Match 1–6 to a–f to complete Mark's sentences.
1. I never drink coffee at home   _c_
2. I always go to bed at 11:30   _____
3. I usually cycle to work,   _____
4. I often watch TV in the evenings,   _____
5. I usually have cornflakes for breakfast,   _____
6. I always get up at seven on weekdays   _____

a   but I sometimes have croissants.
b   but I sometimes take the bus when it rains.
c   because I don't have a coffee machine.
d   because I don't want to be late for work.
e   but on Wednesday evenings I play tennis and on Friday evenings I go to the pub.
f   because I want to sleep for more than seven hours.

9 Put the words in the correct order to make sentences. Which sentences are true for you? Tell a partner.
1. coffee / drink / the / I / morning / sometimes
   I sometimes drink coffee in the morning.
2. to / always / I / walk / work
   _____
3. six o'clock / parents / usually / get up / my / at
   _____
4. never / have / I / breakfast
   _____
5. before / work / have / I / a shower / often
   _____
6. always / I / dinner / have / eight o'clock / at
   _____

10 Work with a partner. Look at Miguel and Laura's week. Make sentences about them.

Miguel and Laura

	get up	bath	breakfast	get home	evening	bed
Mon	7:00	no (shower)	toast	6:00	TV	11:30
Tues	7:00	no (shower)	toast	6:00	TV	11:30
Weds	7:00	no (shower)	toast	6:00	pub	11:30
Thurs	7:00	no (shower)	cornflakes	6:00	TV	11:30
Fri	8:00	no (shower)	cornflakes	6:00	restaurant	11:30

> *They usually get up at seven o'clock.*

> *They sometimes get up at eight o'clock.*

11 Talk to your partner about your routine. Use adverbs of frequency.
- have eggs for breakfast
- go to the cinema
- read a book in the evenings
- get up at six o'clock
- go to bed very late
- go to a café or restaurant
- watch TV in the evenings
- cycle to work
- have a sandwich for lunch
- buy a coffee in a café
- cook for friends

> *I never have eggs for breakfast. I don't like eggs. What about you?*

> *I sometimes have eggs for breakfast in a café.*

12 What is the same about your routine? Tell the class.

We never read a book in the evenings.

6B When do you …?

> Grammar: Present Simple: he/she/it
> Pronunciation: Third person -s
> Vocabulary: Prepositions
> Reading: How famous people start the day
> Listening: Questions and answers

1 Work with a partner. Discuss the questions.
   1 When do you usually get up on weekdays?
   2 When do you usually get up on Saturdays?
   3 What do you usually eat for breakfast?
   I usually get up at six o'clock on weekdays.

2 ⏵091 Read and listen to the text. Write the correct names for photos 1–5.

1 ……………… and ………………   2 ………………

3 ………………   4 ………………

5 ……………… and ………………

3 Read the text again. Look at the underlined verbs. Underline all other verbs in the text. What do you notice about the verb endings?

4 Read the grammar box and check your ideas.

Grammar: Present Simple: he/she/it   ▶ PAGE 93

In the Present Simple, we add **-s** with *he*, *she* or *it*.
I eat breakfast at eight o'clock. > He **eats** breakfast at eight o'clock.
I get up at 7.30. > She **gets** up at 7.30.
If the verb ends in *ch*, *sh*, *ss*, or *x*, add **-es**.
I watch TV. > She **watches** TV.
Some verbs are irregular.
have > he **has**, do > she **does**, go > it **goes**

How FOUR famous people start the day!

Jennifer Aniston, actor
Jennifer Aniston <u>gets up</u> at 4.30 am. She washes her face and then she has a smoothie for breakfast. After that she cycles for half an hour in the gym and then she does yoga for 40 minutes.

Simon Cowell, TV presenter
Simon Cowell <u>wakes up</u> and he drinks a cup of hot water with lemon juice. He eats breakfast in bed – cereal and a fruit smoothie. Then he gets up and he does 150 push-ups or he goes to the gym. After that, he has a bath.

Kate Hudson, actor

Kate Hudson <u>gets up</u> at 7.30 am, she drinks a coffee and watches TV. Then she takes her children to school. After that she does some exercise and then she eats breakfast. She likes eggs, avocado, bacon and tomatoes for breakfast.

Peter Jones, British businessman and entrepreneur

Peter Jones <u>gets up</u> at 6.15, he has a shower and he gets dressed. He eats breakfast and then he leaves home. He buys a coffee – a cappuccino – and he checks his emails on his way to the office.

42

Routines

5 ▶092 Listen to the verbs in the table. What sound is the 's' at the end?

/s/	/z/	/ɪz/
gets (up/dressed)	has	washes
drinks	cycles	
	does	

6 ▶093 Complete the table with the other verbs from the text. Listen and check. Then listen and repeat.

7 Work with a partner. Complete the answers to the questions.
1. What does Jennifer Aniston do for 40 minutes?
   She ___does___ yoga.
2. Where does Simon Cowell eat breakfast?
   He .... breakfast in bed.
3. What time does Jennifer Aniston get up?
   She .... at 4.30 am.
4. Does Peter Jones buy a smoothie?
   No, he doesn't buy a smoothie. He .... a coffee.
5. Does Peter Jones have a bath in the mornings?
   No, he doesn't have a bath. He .... a shower.
6. Does Kate Hudson take her children to school?
   ...., she does.
7. Does Simon Cowell eat eggs for breakfast?
   ...., he doesn't.
8. Does Kate Hudson watch TV in the mornings?
   Yes, she............ .

8 ▶094 Listen and check. Then complete the grammar box with *does* or *doesn't*.

> **Grammar: Present Simple negatives and questions: he, she, it** ▶ PAGE 93
>
> For negatives with *he/she/it*, we use ¹............ (*does not*) + verb.
> He **doesn't have** a bath.
>
> For questions with *he/she/it*, we use ²............ + *he/she/it* + verb. We use *does* or ³............ in short answers.
> '**Does he buy** a smoothie?' 'Yes, he **does**.' 'No, he **doesn't**.'
>
> We can also use questions words (*Where, What, Who*, etc.). Look at the word order.
> **Where does he eat** breakfast?
> **What** time **does she get up**?

9 Complete the questions with the correct form of the verbs in brackets. Then ask and answer the questions with a partner.
1. ___Does___ Jennifer Aniston ___have___ cereal for breakfast? (have)
2. What .... Simon Cowell .... when he first wakes up? (drink)
3. How many push-ups .... he ....? (do)
4. .... Kate Hudson .... at 8.30? (get up)
5. What .... she .... for breakfast? (like)
6. What .... Peter Jones .... before he leaves home? (do)

> Does Jennifer Aniston have cereal for breakfast?

> No, she doesn't. She has a smoothie.

10 Complete the table with *on*, *in* and *at*.

1	the weekend, eleven o'clock, a quarter past three
2	Wednesday, Friday evening, Saturday morning, Tuesday afternoon
3	the morning, the afternoon, the evening

11 Work with a partner. Ask and answer the questions.
When do you … do exercise / drink coffee / start work or school / meet friends?

> When do you do exercise?

> I do exercise on Saturday mornings.

12 Tell your partner the names of two people in your family. Use the prompts to ask questions about them.
- What / .... / do at the weekend?
- What time / .... usually / get up / on Mondays?
- What / .... usually / do / in the evenings?
- Where / .... / work or study?
- What / .... / usually / eat / for breakfast?
- What exercise .... / do?

> What does Julie do at the weekend?

> She goes to the gym and she …

43

6C In a hotel

▶ **Speaking:** Checking into a hotel; Asking about facilities
▶ **Writing:** Filling in a form; Dates, postcodes and phone numbers

Speaking

1 Work with a partner. Match the pictures of things in a hotel to the words.

> swimming pool   breakfast   lift   WiFi   gym

1 ....

2 ....

3 ....

4 ....

5 ....

2 ▶ 095 Listen, check and repeat.

3 Which things in exercise 1 are important to you when you stay in a hotel? Number them 1 (very important) to 5 (not important). Compare answers with your partner.

4 ▶ 096 Julie wants to check into a hotel. Listen and number the words in the order you hear them.

> gym   WiFi   dining room
> form   password   breakfast   lift
> key card   swimming pool

5 ▶ 096 Listen again and answer the questions.
1 What is Julie's surname?
2 What is her room number and where is it?
3 What time is breakfast?
4 Does the hotel have a swimming pool?
5 What time does the gym open?

6 ▶ 097 Complete the sentences in the *Key Language* box with the words in the box. Then listen, check and repeat.

> open   in   welcome   ~~Can~~   there   Here's
> What   served   on   at   Does

KEY LANGUAGE   Checking into a hotel

What the guest says
1 *Can* I check into my room, please?
Is ² .... WiFi in my room?
³ .... time is breakfast?
⁴ .... the hotel have a gym?
What time does the gym ⁵ ....?

What the receptionist says
Can you fill ⁶ .... this form, please?
You're in room 302 ⁷ .... the third floor.
⁸ .... your key card.
Breakfast is ⁹ .... from seven until ten.
It opens ¹⁰ .... six o'clock in the morning.
You're ¹¹ .... Enjoy your stay.

7 Match the questions and answers. Then practise them with a partner.
1 Does the hotel have a swimming pool?
2 What time is breakfast?
3 Can you fill in this form, please?
4 Is there WiFi in my room?
5 Can I check in, please?
6 Thanks for your help.

a Yes. The password and login are in your room.
b Of course. What's your name?
c Yes, of course.
d Yes, it does.
e It's served from six until nine thirty.
f You're welcome. Enjoy your stay.

🌱 YOUR TURN

8 Work with a partner. Student A turn to page 99. Student B turn to page 103.

9 Repeat the conversations in exercise 7. This time use your own names and ask different questions.

44

Routines

Writing

1 Work in small groups. Discuss the questions.
   1 What information does a hotel usually want from a guest?
   2 Do hotels in your country often take …
      • your credit card?
      • your passport?
      • your car keys?

2 Complete the hotel form with information from the ID card and the numbers in the box.

NAME
Toby Banks
DATE OF BIRTH
24-05-1997
PLACE OF BIRTH
Great Britain
ADDRESS
24 Blake Close, Cambridge, CB1 6DY

+44 7792 5444113   31.05.21   02.06.21
290297845

Welcome to the Warton hotel
Please fill in this registration form.

First name: [1]
Surname: [2]
Postcode: [3]
City: [4]
Phone: [5]
Email: *t_banks@tmail.com*
Passport number: [6]
Nationality: [7]
Signature: *Toby Banks*
Date of arrival: [8]
Date of departure: [9]
Method of payment: *Credit card*
Check in from 2 pm.
Check out time is 11 am.
Breakfast is from 7–10 am.

3 Choose the correct words to complete the *Key Language* box.

KEY LANGUAGE Dates, postcodes and phone numbers

Dates
In Britain people write the [1]*day / month*, then the [2]*day / month*, then the year.
31.05.21 (= May 31, 2021)
In US English, the [3]*day / month* is first.
05.31.21 (= May 31, 2021)

Postcodes
In UK addresses, postcodes come [4]*before / after* the city: *24 Blake Close, Cambridge, CB1 6DY*

In other countries, they often come before the city: *10405 Berlin*

International phone code
Add 0044 (+44) [5]*before / after* a UK phone number.

4 Answer the questions. Then compare your answers with a partner.
   1 Write today's date in British English and then in American English.
   2 How do you write dates in your country? Write the date of your birthday this year.
   3 What is your postcode? Does it come before or after the city in your country?
   4 What is the international phone code for your country?

YOUR TURN

5 Work with a partner. Student A turn to page 99. Student B turn to page 104.

Video 3: Two different routines

3: Two different routines

1 Work with a partner. Discuss the questions.
   1 What clothes shops do you like? Why?
   2 In your country, are clothes shops open …
      • at 8.00 am?
      • on Sundays?
      • after 8.00 pm?

2 Read about shop opening times in four different countries. Answer the questions.
   1 In two countries, some supermarkets are always open. Which countries?
   2 What time do shops open on Sundays in the UK?
   3 In which country do shops close at lunchtime?
   4 Are clothes shops open in Germany on Sundays?
   5 In three countries, you can shop until 10 pm. Which countries?

3 Work with a partner. Which country has the best opening times? Why?

SHOP OPENING times

UK
- Shops are open every day. They usually open at 9 and close at 5 or 6 pm.
- On Sundays, shops often open at 11 am and close at 4 or 5 pm.
- Some supermarkets never close!

Germany
- Clothes shops aren't open on Sundays in Germany.
- They are open on all other days – usually from 8 am until 8 pm.

Spain
- Shops are open from 8:30 or 9 am. until 1:30 pm. They open again from 4:30 until 7.30 or 8 pm.
- Some shops stay open until 10 pm.
- Some big shopping malls are open on Sundays, but small shops are often closed.

Singapore
- Shops are usually open from 10 am until 10 pm.
- Some supermarkets are open 24 hours a day, every day!

4 ▶ Watch the video. Number the things in the order you find out about them.
  a toast ....
  b football ....
  c TV ....
  d biscuits ....
  e chocolate ....

5 ▶ Watch the video again. Choose the correct words to complete the sentences.
  1 Ramon's city is *Edinburgh / Cadiz*.
  2 Catriona works in a department store in *Scotland / Spain*.
  3 Ramon gets up at *6.30 am / 8.30 am*.
  4 Catriona starts work at *7.30 am / 9.00 am*.
  5 Catriona has *some biscuits / a sandwich* at 1 pm.
  6 *Ramon / Catriona* sleeps after lunch.
  7 After work, *Ramon / Catriona* usually goes to a bar.
  8 Ramon goes to bed at *11 / midnight*.

6 Work with a partner. Discuss the questions.
  1 Which breakfast do you like best: coffee and cake (Ramon) or cereal, toast and tea (Catriona)?
  2 What does Ramon usually have for lunch? What about Catriona? What do you usually have?
  3 Which routine do you like best? Ramon's or Catriona's? Why?

Review

LESSON 5A We *play board games, go shopping* and *do yoga*. What other activities do we *play, go* and *do*?

LESSON 5A Write 2 sentences about activities you do and activities you don't do.

LESSON 5B Write 3 Present Simple questions. For example: *Do you live in London?*

LESSON 5B Write short answers about you to these questions: *Do you eat Mexican food? Do you speak Russian?*

LESSON 5C Write 5 questions using the question words: *What, When, Where, Who, Which*.

LESSON 5C Write 2 sentences about you. In one sentence use *and*, in the other use *because*.

LESSON 6A Write about your routine on a Monday morning.

LESSON 6A What do you often do? What do you never do? Write two sentences.

LESSON 6B What is the Present Simple *he/she/it* form of *do, wash, drink,* and *have*?

LESSON 6B Do we use *on, in* or *at* with these words: *10 o'clock, the evening, Friday*?

LESSON 6C Write 3 questions to ask a hotel receptionist when you check in.

LESSON 6C What is your surname? What is your postcode?

7 Free time

- **Vocabulary:** *Free-time activities*
- **Grammar:** *Like / love / hate + -ing*
- **Listening:** *My friends*
- **Reading:** *#metime*

7A What do you like doing?

1 Match the pictures to the activities in the box.

> going out   staying at home   walking   relaxing
> meeting friends   travelling   playing the piano
> eating out

2 🎧 099 Listen and check. What other activities do you like doing?

3 Read the profiles. Complete them with verbs from exercise 1.

4 Which people do you think are friends? Why? Choose two pairs.

> *I think … and … are friends because they both like …*

MIA
I love food and seeing friends. I like cooking Italian food and I love **¹** .... out to bars and restaurants with friends. I like being outside and I love **²** .... my dog. I hate flying.

LISA
I love doing exercise and I go to the gym a lot. I like walking in the countryside but I really don't like walking in the city. I like cooking and **³** .... out with friends is one of my favourite activities.

ANA
I love **⁴** .... friends for lunch or a coffee. I also like shopping with my friends. I really like spending time with people and I hate **⁵** .... at home!

HARRY
I like doing exercise and I really love running and cycling. It's really relaxing. I love food and I like eating out, but I hate cooking. I'm a terrible cook!

SAM
I love cooking. I really enjoy cooking Italian food. In my free time I like going to the cinema. For holidays, I always stay in the UK. I don't like **⁶** .... to other countries, and I hate flying.

TOM
I love having meals with friends. Good food and chatting with friends are my favourite activities. I like travelling and every year I go to a new country. I hate watching TV. When I'm at home I like **⁷** .... the piano and relaxing.

Free time

5 ▶100 Listen and complete the sentences. What do the people like doing together?

1 **Mia** My best friend is .... We often go on holiday together. We always go to a place with a good ....

2 **Tom** My best friends are .... and .... We often go on .... together.

3 **Lisa** My best friend is my boyfriend .... We often go to the .... together.

6 Read the grammar box and complete it with the correct verb forms.

> **Grammar:** *Like/love/hate* + verb +*-ing*   ▶ PAGE 94
>
> We can use *like*, *love*, *hate*, etc. + a noun or a verb + *-ing*:
> I **love** food. I **love** cooking.
>
> **Spelling**
> When a one-syllable verb ends in *-e* we usually remove the *-e* and add *-ing*.
> I **have** meals with my friends. I like ¹ .... meals with my friends.
> I **cycle** a lot. I love ² ....
>
> With some vowels that end with a vowel + consonant, we double the consonant and add *-ing*.
> I **travel** a lot. I love ³ .... to other countries.
> I don't **swim** very often. I hate ⁴ .... in the sea!

7 Write sentences. Use the correct form of *like* or *love* and the *-ing* form of the verb in brackets.

1 I / like / travel — *I don't like travelling.*
2 I / love / read + ...
3 you / like / swim ? ....
4 she / like / cycle − ....
5 he / love / play the piano + ...
6 they / like / walk ? ....
7 I / like / go out with friends + ...

8 Work with a partner. Look at the pictures in exercise 1. Tell your partner about the activities you like and don't like. Use *me too* and *me neither* when you agree.

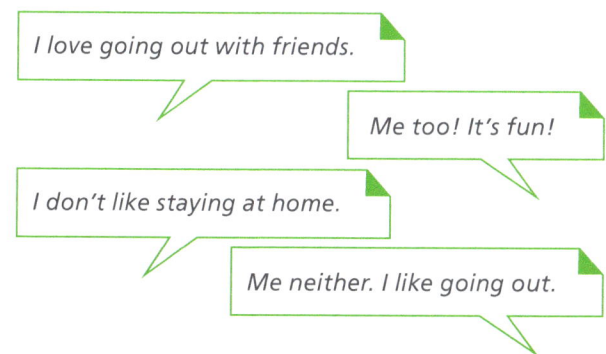

> I love going out with friends.
>
> Me too! It's fun!
>
> I don't like staying at home.
>
> Me neither. I like going out.

9 Read the tweets. Complete the sentences.

1 Gelson and Meiko both like ....
2 Piotr only likes .... and .... when he isn't tired.
3 Samantha and Chang both like ....
4 Samantha likes cycling in any weather but Chang doesn't like cycling in the ....
5 .... are Nori's favourite type of film.
6 .... helps Maria to relax.

#metime

 Samantha
What do you like doing when you have time just for you? I love walking or cycling in the countryside. I like it in the sun, rain, snow – any weather! #metime

 Gelson
I love sitting down with a cup of coffee and reading the news and social media on my phone! I also love chatting with my friends on the phone. #metime

 Piotr
It depends. When I am tired, I like sitting at home and relaxing in front of the TV. When I have a lot of energy, I like running or swimming. I love swimming in the sea! #metime

 Chang
I usually take the car to work, but I don't really like driving. When I'm not busy, I like cycling to work. I don't do it very often because it's fifteen kilometres and I hate cycling in the rain! #metime

 Nori
I love going to the cinema with my children. I really enjoy watching cartoons. They are my favourite type of film. I'm a big child! #metime

 Meiko
I like sitting in the garden and reading a book. I also love falling asleep in the garden in the sun. When I have money, I love shopping. #metime

 Maria
I like doing housework! It's fun! All my friends think I'm a bit strange because of it. 🙂 #metime

---

10 Which person likes similar things to you? Compare your choice with a partner.

11 Write a tweet for the hashtag #metime. Give your tweet to the teacher. Play 'Guess whose tweet it is.'

49

7B My favourites

▸ **Grammar:** Word order in questions
▸ **Reading:** An interview
▸ **Pronunciation:** 'Do you' in questions

1 Work with a partner. Ask and answer the questions about the things in the box. Give a reason.

> food   drink   sport   song   film   TV programme
> town or city   sport

What's your favourite city?

My favourite city is New York. It's exciting!

2 Look at the interview and pictures. Who is Harriet Simpson?

3 Read the interview. Complete the sentences with the correct words.
   1 .... is Harriet's favourite city.
   2 Harriet is married to ....
   3 Her husband is a ....
   4 She loves music by ....
   5 Nicholas Britell puts classical music with .... music.
   6 Freddie and Ella are Harriet's .... and ....
   7 At the moment Harriet is on ....
   8 She does .... shows each year.

HARRIET SIMPSON, MUSICIAN

Q & A

Tom from London
Hi, Harriet! You're from London, but you don't live here. So, where do you live?

Harriet Hi, Tom! You're right, I am from London. I live in Vienna. I work in Central Europe a lot. Vienna is my favourite city. It's an amazing place!

Chang South Korea
Who are you married to? And what does your husband do?

Harriet Hi, Chang. I'm married to Andreas. He's from Austria. He's a musician like me. He plays the cello.

Ana from Portugal
I love your music. Your new album is amazing. Who is your favourite musician?

Harriet I love Nicholas Britell. He writes music for a lot of TV shows and films. He puts really unusual styles of music together. Classical music with hip hop! It's so different to listen to.

Nori from Japan
I love your social media posts. The children are really cute! Are they your children? How old are they?

Harriet Thank you! They are my sister's children, my nephew and niece – Freddie and Ella. They are eight and ten years old.

Hank from the US
When are you on tour again? Do you like touring in the US?

Harriet I'm on tour at the moment. I love touring in the US!

Piotr from Poland
How many shows do your do every year? And why do you like being a musician?

Harriet I do 30 or 40 shows every year. The thing I really love is travelling!

Free time

4 Complete the questions with the words in the box. Check in the interview.

> are   do   how many   what
> when   where   who (x 2)   why

1 .... do you live?
2 .... are you married to?
3 .... does your husband do?
4 .... is your favourite musician?
5 .... they your children?
6 .... are you on tour again?
7 .... you plan to play in the US again?
8 .... shows do you do every year?
9 .... do you like being a musician?

5 Work with a partner. Ask and answer the questions.

- Where are you from?
- Who do you live with?
- What do you do?
- How old are you?
- Are you married?
- How many children do you have?

6 Read the grammar box. Complete it with the correct words.

Grammar: Word order in questions ▶ PAGE 94

Questions with be
The position of the verb *be* changes in questions.

+	?
He's American.	Is he American?
You ¹................ 28 years old.	How old ²................ you?

Present simple questions

+	?
You speak English.	Do you speak English?
He lives in the USA.	³................ he .... in the USA?

Look at the word order when there is a question word.
What do you do?
Where ⁴................ she live?

7 Put the words in the correct order to make questions.
1 married / is / he ?
2 they / busy / are ?
3 you / have / do / a sister or brother?
4 Chinese food / you / like / do ?
5 like / what music / you / do ?
6 go to the gym / you / when / do ?

8 ▶ 101 Listen to four of the questions from exercise 7. Notice how the people say *do you*. Listen again and repeat.

9 Complete the questions with *is*, *are*, *do* or *does*.
1 Where .... your sister live?
2 What .... you think?
3 .... you hungry? Let's have lunch.
4 How old .... your mum?
5 .... you like hip hop music?
6 .... football your favourite sport?
7 What TV programmes .... your dad like watching?
8 .... we late for class?

10 Complete the questions. Then write answers that are true for you.
1 what time / you finish work or school?
2 what time / you have dinner?
3 what / you do / in the evenings?
4 you do / sport or exercise at the weekend?
5 you go out / at the weekend? Where / you go?
6 where / you have lunch on Sundays?
7 what / your favourite shop?
8 you tired / on Friday evenings?

11 Work with a partner. Ask and answer the questions in exercise 10.

12 Work with a new partner. Ask and answer questions about your first partner.

> What time does Marco finish work?

> He usually finishes at six o'clock.

7C Travel

> - **Speaking:** At the train station
> - **Vocabulary:** Travel
> - **Writing:** A description of a day; Time sequencers

Speaking

1 Work with a partner. Ask and answer the questions.
   1 Do you sometimes go away at the weekend?
   2 Where do you go?
   3 How do you like travelling? Why?
      - by train • by bus • by car

2 ▶102 Match the words in the box to the pictures. Listen and check.

> passenger   platform   ticket
> ticket machine   ticket office

3 ▶103 Listen to a conversation at a train station. Choose the correct answers.
   1 The woman wants … .
      a a single   b a return   c two returns
   2 She wants a ticket for … .
      a today   b tomorrow   c today and tomorrow
   3 The ticket costs … .
      a 49 euros   b 39 euros   c 29 euros
   4 The next train is at … .
      a 14:15   b 14:50   c 14:45
   5 The train arrives in Paris at … .
      a 16.15   b 16:30   c 16:40

4 ▶103 Complete the *Key Language* box with the words in the box. Listen again and check.

> come   does   next   platform
> please   return   to

KEY LANGUAGE   At the train station

A ticket [1] ………………… Paris, please.
Single or [2] …………………?
A return, [3] ………………….
When do you want to [4] ………………… back?
What time is the [5] ………………… train?
The train leaves from [6] ………………… 5.
What time [7] ………………… it arrive in Paris?

Note: We usually use the 24-hour clock for train, bus and plane times. *The train leaves at 16:30.*

5 Match the questions to the answers.
   1 Single or return?
   2 How much is a return to Amsterdam?
   3 What time is the next train?
   4 Which platform is it?
   5 When does the train arrive?

   a The next train is at 8:35.
   b 68 euros.
   c It gets in at 9:57.
   d A single, please.
   e Number 3.

YOUR TURN

6 Work in pairs. Student A turn to page 100. Student B use the information below.
   A Ask questions to complete the table.

Ticket	A single to Venice
Price	
Time of the next train	
Platform	
Arrival time	

   B Use the information to answer your partner's questions.

Ticket	A return to Lyon
Price	65 euros
Time of the next train	13: 28
Platform	2
Arrival time	15: 42

My life

Writing

1 Match the activities in the pictures to the words in the box.

> cooking a meal   getting a takeaway   lying in bed
> visiting family   walking in the countryside

2 Which things in exercise 1 do you like doing? Compare your ideas with a partner.

3 Read the blog post and comments from the magazine *My Life*. Underline the activities that Michael and Heidi like doing.

4 Find these words in the blog. Then use them to complete the *Key Language* box.

> after that   first   then   finally

KEY LANGUAGE   Time sequencers

We use ¹ .... to talk about an activity at the start of something.
We use ² .... and ³ .... to talk about activities that come next.
We use ⁴ .... to talk about the last activity.
Note when we use *First, After that* and ⁵ .... at the beginning of a sentence, we use a comma after them.

5 Look at the four activities Marta likes doing. Use the words in the *Key Language* box to say when she likes doing them.

1 walk in the countryside
2 lunch in a pub
3 visit my parents
4 watch a film

First, Marta likes…

YOUR TURN

6 Write a description of your perfect Saturday. Use words in the *Key Language* box to say when you like doing the activities.

7 Work in groups. Read the other descriptions. Which ones are similar to yours?

My perfect SATURDAY

In the *My Life* office we all love lying in bed on a Saturday morning, then meeting friends in the afternoon and finally getting a takeaway to have in front of Netflix in the evening. What do you love doing on a Saturday? Tell us about your perfect Saturday!

MICHAEL
First, I like lying in bed. Then I have a coffee and read the news online. After that, I visit my parents. Finally, I order my favourite takeaway – pizza!

HEIDI
First, I get up early and go for a run. I hate lying in bed! Then I go shopping with friends and after that we usually have lunch together. Finally, in the evening, I usually go out for dinner or drinks with my boyfriend.

8 Eat, play, shop

- **Vocabulary:** Food
- **Pronunciation:** Sounds and spelling
- **Grammar:** Some and any
- **Listening:** What food do you like?
- **Reading:** Famous people and food

8A The food I like

1. Work with a partner. Match the pictures to the foods in the box.

   > apples   avocado   bananas   beef   bread
   > broccoli   cheese   chicken   cucumber   eggs
   > ham   lettuce   onions   pasta   potatoes
   > rice   salmon   sausages   strawberries   tomatoes

2. 105 Listen, check and repeat. Do you know any other foods in English?

3. Complete the table with food from exercise 1.

Vegetables	
Fruit	
Meat and fish	
Other	

4. ▶106 Listen to some of the words again. Underline the sound you CAN'T hear in each one.
   1. strawberries
   2. vegetables
   3. salmon

5. ▶107 Listen to a conversation between Louisa and Ken. Where do they decide to have dinner?
   1. at Louisa's house
   2. at Ken's house
   3. at a restaurant

54

Eat, play, shop

6 ▶107 Listen again. What food does Ken like? What food does Louisa like? Write K or L next to the words in the box.

> apples avocado beef cheese chicken
> cucumber eggs fruit lettuce pasta
> potatoes rice strawberries vegetables

7 Work with a partner. Ask and answer questions about the food in exercise 1.

> Do you like cheese?
>
> Yes, I do. I love cheese!
>
> Me, too.

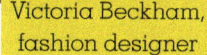
Victoria Beckham, fashion designer

Mo Farah, athlete

Boris Johnson, politician

Meghan Markle, actress

Prince Charles

8 Read the article about five famous people. Match the pictures 1–5 to the people A–E.

What do FAMOUS people eat?

Person A: Every day, this person has a four-minute egg and some tea with milk for breakfast. A doesn't eat any food for lunch!

Person B: This person has avocado on toast with some olive oil for breakfast.

Person C: This person loves sausages and eats them with some potatoes. And C drinks a litre of diet cola every day!

Person D: This person often has a chicken sandwich for lunch, then some fruit in the afternoon and usually salmon with some vegetables for dinner.

Person E: Does this person eat any cheese? No, but E eats some fish (usually sushi) every day.

9 Work with a partner. Look at the five famous people. Who do you think each person in the article is?

10 ▶108 Listen and check.

11 Find examples of *some* and *any* in the article. in exercise 8. Complete the grammar box with *some* or *any*.

> **Grammar:** *Some* and *any*   ▶ PAGE 94
>
> We use ¹................. in positive sentences:
> He has **some** tea with milk.
> We use ²................. with questions and negatives.
> He doesn't eat **any** food for lunch.
> 'Does she eat **any** cheese?' 'No, she doesn't.' 'Yes, she does.'

12 ▶109 Complete the conversations with *some* or *any*. Then listen and check. Practise the conversations with a partner.

1. **A:** What would you like to drink?
   B: I'd like .... water please.
2. **A:** Do you have .... cheese?
   B: Yes. We have .... cheddar.
3. **A:** Which sandwich would you like? Ham or chicken?
   B: I don't eat .... meat. Do you have .... cheese sandwiches?
4. **A:** Do you have .... coffee?
   B: No, we don't. But we have .... tea.
5. **A:** I don't have .... lettuce for the salad, but I have .... tomatoes and .... cucumber.
   B: Do you have .... avocados?

13 Work with a partner. Student A turn to page 100. Student B turn to page 104.

8B Yes, I can!

- **Grammar:** Can and can't
- **Vocabulary:** Adverbs
- **Reading:** My daughter – the art student
- **Listening:** Questions and answers

1. Work with a partner. Look at the pictures. Complete the sentences with verbs in the box.

> sing ride play lift dance drive swim speak

1 He can __ride__ a bike.   2 She can _____.

3 He can _____.   4 He can _____ 100 kilos.

5 She can _____.   6 He can _____ the piano.

7 She can _____ Russian.   8 She can _____ a bus.

2. ▶110 Listen and check. Notice how we say 'can'. Listen again and repeat.

3. Tick the things that you can do.

I CAN …
- swim ✓   dance   sing   drive a car
- ride …   a bike / a motorbike
- play …   the piano / the guitar / the violin / (other)
- speak … Russian / French / Spanish / (other)
- lift …   100kgs / 60kgs / 20kgs / (other)

4. Work with a partner. Take turns to tell your partner what you can do.

> I can swim and I can play the piano. And you?

> I can speak Spanish and I can lift 60 kilos.

5. Look at the pictures of Lisa in the article. Which of the following do you think Lisa can do?
   ride a bike / paint / cook / sing

6. ▶111 Read and listen to the article and check your ideas.

7. Read the article again and answer the questions.
   1. What does Lisa study?
   2. Who is Emma?
   3. What does Emma cook for them?
   4. Why is it easy to travel around in Glasgow?
   5. What is the name of Lisa and Emma's band?

My DAUGHTER – the art student

My daughter, Lisa, is a student. She studies Art at the Glasgow School of Art in Scotland. She is really good at art and she can paint really well. She loves Spanish artists – especially Picasso, and she can speak Spanish fluently!

But university isn't always easy for Lisa. She can't cook at all, so she eats a lot of pizzas and takeaways! Her best friend, Emma, can cook a little bit, so sometimes they eat pasta or sausages with potatoes and vegetables.

Lisa can't drive, so she always travels by bus or train. She can ride a bike quite well, but she doesn't like cycling. It's good that there is a subway in Glasgow, so it's easy to travel around.

She's in a band called *The Celestinas* with Emma and two other friends. Lisa can't sing at all, but she can play the guitar really well and Emma is a great singer, so the band is quite good! I love watching them play.

Eat, play, shop

8 Read the grammar box. Complete the sentences with *can* or *can't*.

> **Grammar:** *can* and *can't* ▶ PAGE 94
>
> *Can* and *can't* have the same form for *I / you / he / she / it / we / they*.
>
> **Positive:**
>
> I **can** drive. You **can** drive. She **can** drive. We **can** drive. They ¹............ drive.
>
> **Negative:**
>
> I **can't** drive. You **can't** drive. She ².............. drive. We **can't** drive. They **can't** drive.
>
> **Questions:**
>
> Can you drive? Yes, I ³............. . No, I ⁴............. .

9 🔊 112 Complete the questions and answers about Lisa. Then listen and check.
1. 'Can Lisa __paint__?' '__Yes__, she can. She __can__ paint really well.'
2. '............ she speak Spanish?' 'Yes, she .... She can .... Spanish fluently.'
3. 'Can she ....?' '............, she can't. She .... cook at all.'
4. '............ she drive?' 'No, she ....'
5. 'Can she .... a bike?' '............, she can. She .... ride a bike quite well.'
6. '............ she sing?' '............, she can't. She can't .... at all.'
7. 'Can she .... the guitar?' 'Yes, she .... She .... play the guitar really well.'

10 🔊 113 Listen to these sentences. How do the people say *can* and *can't* in each sentence?
1. She can paint really well.
2. She can't cook at all.
3. 'Can she drive?' 'No, she can't.'
4. 'Can she play the guitar?' 'Yes, she can.'

11 Practise the questions and answers in exercise 9 with a partner.

12 Find and underline the adverbs in the box in the article. Then match them to the pictures.

> really well   fluently   not at all
> quite well   a (little) bit

1 ...., ...
2 ...., ...
3 ....

13 Work with a partner. Answer the questions.
1. Do adverbs go before or after the verb in a sentence?
2. Which adverb is about languages?

14 Walk around the class and talk to other students. Find out what they can do. Write their names.

> Can you speak Italian?
>
> Yes, I can. I can speak Italian quite well. Can you speak Italian?
>
> No. I can't speak Italian at all!

Find someone who can …

	✓ really well	✓ quite well	✓ a little bit
speak Italian			
cook			
play football			
play golf			
sing			
dance			
play the piano			
ride a horse			
paint			

8C Making requests

> **Speaking:** Shopping
> **Writing:** A text message; Making requests and giving answers

Speaking

1 Work in small groups. Discuss the questions.
   1 Where do you like shopping for food?

   > at the supermarket   at the market
   > at small shops   online

   2 How often do you shop for food?
   3 How much does your food shopping cost per week?

2 ▶114 Listen to three conversations in shops. Write the conversation number next to the foods. Which food does the shop NOT have?
   a cheddar cheese ....
   b ham ....
   c onions ....
   d avocados ....
   e salmon ....

3 ▶114 Complete the *Key Language* box with words from the box. Listen again and check.

   > any   Can   else   grams   How
   > I'd   of   piece   three   would

KEY LANGUAGE Shopping

Asking for things
¹............ I have some ... , please?
Can I have 500 grams ²............ ... , please?
Do you have ³............ ... ?
⁴............ like three pieces of ... , please.

Amounts
a small ⁵............   100 ⁶............   ⁷............ pieces

Serving customers
⁸............ can I help you?   How many ⁹............ you like?
Anything ¹⁰............ ?

4 Put the words in the correct order to make sentences. Then match 1–5 with a–e.
   1 some / I / have / please / bananas / can / ?
   ....
   2 a / please / I'd / like / piece / small / beef / of /
   ....
   3 rice / you / any / do / have / ?
   ....
   4 I / how / you / can / help / ? ....
   5 else / you / like / would / anything / ?
   ....

   a No, thanks.
   b No, we don't. Sorry.
   c Can I have some tomatoes, please?
   d Sure. How many would you like?
   e Of course. Is 500 grams OK?

5 Work with a partner. Practise the questions and answers in exercise 4.

YOUR TURN

6 Work with a partner. Student A turn to page 101. Student B turn to page 105.

7 Write a shopping list with four kinds of food you often buy. Work with a new partner. Use your lists and take turns to be the customer and the shop worker.

Shopping list

58

Eat, play, shop

Writing

1 Work with a partner. Discuss the questions.
   1 How do you send messages? Do you use WhatsApp, Facebook messenger or normal SMS? Why?
   2 Read about text messaging in Britain. Is it the same or different in your country? How many messages do you get each day?

TEXT or *talk*?
- Many British people get over 90 messages a day on their phones!
- 18-24-year-olds get the most – over 230 messages per day!
- Young British people like messages more than phone calls.

2 Read the text messages from Nick and Helen. Answer the questions.
   1 Who does Nick want to invite to dinner?
   2 Where does Nick ask Helen to go?
   3 What does he want to cook?
   4 When can Helen go shopping?
   5 Why doesn't Helen want any more messages?

3 Read the Key Language box. Complete it with the phrases in the box.

> Sure, no problem.
> I have a meeting.   Can you do something for me?

KEY LANGUAGE Making requests

Making requests
Can you invite … to … ?   Can you go to … ?
1 ....

Answering requests
Of course I can.   Sorry, I can't.   2 ....

Giving reasons
I'm at work.   I don't have time.   3 ....

4 Rewrite the underlined sentences. Use phrases from the Key Language box.
   1 A: Can you buy some bread today?
      B: <u>No</u>. I'm at school. ....
   2 A: Can you cook dinner tonight?
      B: <u>Yes</u>. ....
   3 A: <u>Go to the supermarket today.</u>
      ....
      B: Sure, no problem. What would you like?
   4 A: Can you do something for me?
      B: What?
      A: <u>Take the dog for a walk.</u> ....
      A: <u>Yes</u>. ....

YOUR TURN

5 Work with a partner. Think of two requests for your partner. Then:
   1 Write a message to your partner on a piece of paper. Make your first request. Give the message to your partner.
   2 Read your partner's message. Write an answer to their request. Give it back to your partner.
   3 Write another message to your partner. Make your second request. Give it to your partner.
   4 Write an answer to your partner's second request.

6 Think of a friend who speaks English. Send a message in English to this friend. Make a request.

59

Video 4: Food around the world

4 Food around the world

1 Work with a partner. Discuss the questions.
   1 Which supermarkets are popular in your country?
   2 What takeaway food do you like? How often do you eat takeaway food?
   3 How often do you eat out in restaurants?

2 Read the text. Underline the foods in the text.

3 Read the text again and answer the questions.
   1 Where do lots of Italian people buy vegetables, bread and meat?
   2 Are all supermarkets in Germany the same?
   3 Where do people often go for breakfast in Germany?
   4 Where do some people eat lunch in Germany?
   5 What foods are very fresh in Chinese markets?
   6 When do the markets open in China?
   7 Is online food shopping popular in China?
   8 Which shops are often expensive in the UK?

4 ▶ Watch the video. Tick ✓ the countries or regions in the video.

America	Hong Kong	European Union	Italy
	Japan	the UK	

Food shopping around the world

ITALY
In Italy, lots of people buy food in local shops or at markets. They buy fruit and vegetables at the greengrocer's, bread at the bakery and meat at the butcher's.

GERMANY
In Germany, there are lots of different supermarkets. Some supermarkets are cheap and do not have a lot of different things. Other supermarkets are more expensive. They have lots of things to choose from. For breakfast lots of people buy bread in a bakery. For lunch, many people eat at work in a canteen.

CHINA
In China, many people shop at markets. The fish and meat are very fresh in these markets. These markets sometimes open early – at 5 am. Online shopping is also very popular in China.

UK
Supermarkets in the UK are often very big. They are sometimes open 24 hours a day. There are not very many small food shops like greengrocer's and bakeries. Small food shops are often quite expensive.

5 ▶ **Watch the video again. Complete the sentences about food around the world.**
1 The American family usually eat fish, ..., salad and bread together on a Sunday.
2 In the UK, people spend £ .... billion on food every year.
3 Nowadays people don't buy .... in a bakery, or .... in a butcher's.
4 In the UK, people spend £ .... billion in supermarkets every year.
5 The family in Hong Kong are eating dumplings and .... together.
6 Many people can't ...., so they buy takeaway food and eat out in restaurants.
7 .... million Americans buy fast food every day.
8 Lots of people like eating .... with friends when they watch TV.

6 **Work with a partner. Answer the questions.**
1 Which food shops are expensive in your country? Which are cheap?
2 What fast food do you like? Do you eat a lot of fast food?
3 What's your favourite restaurant? Why?

> *I often shop in supermarkets because they are cheap.*

Review

LESSON 7A	Name 3 activities you like doing in your free time.
LESSON 7A	Write 3 sentences about things you like, love and hate doing.
LESSON 7B	Write one question with the verb *be*. Write another question in the Present Simple.
LESSON 7C	Write 3 useful phrases to use in a train station.
LESSON 7C	Write about your usual morning before school, university or work. Use *first*, *then*, *after that* and *finally*.
LESSON 8A	Name 2 fruits, 2 vegetables and 2 kinds of meat.
LESSON 8A	Use *some* and *any* to write 2 sentences about food you have at home.
LESSON 8B	Write one sentence about something you can do, and one sentence about something you can't do.
LESSON 8B	Use adverbs to write sentences about how well you can speak a language and play an instrument.
LESSON 8C	Write 2 questions to ask for things in a shop.
LESSON 8C	A friend texts you to meet in a café. You can't go. Write a reply and say why you can't go.

9 Out and about

- **Vocabulary:** Verb + noun collocations
- **Grammar:** Present Continuous
- **Listening:** A phone call home

9A What are they doing?

1 Work with a partner. Complete the collocations with the verbs in the box. Then match them to the pictures.

do   message   ~~take~~   work   clean   cook

- A **take** a selfie
- .... my bedroom
- .... on a laptop
- .... dinner
- .... homework
- .... friends

2 ▶116 Listen, check and repeat.

3 Choose the correct words to complete the sentences.
1 I *do / make* two hours of English homework every week.
2 When I get home in the evenings I *work / cook* on my laptop.
3 I *clean / take* my bedroom every weekend.
4 On Sundays I *cook / work* dinner for my family.
5 When I am on holiday I *do / take* lots of selfies.
6 I *message / talk* friends when I wake up in the morning.

4 Work with a partner. Are the sentences in exercise 3 true for you? Tell your partner.

> I don't do two hours of English homework every week. I do one hour! What about you?

> I don't do any English homework!

5 ▶117 Listen to a conversation between Nicola and her husband, Jamie. Where is each person? Match the places in the box to the people.

dining room   hotel   bedroom   kitchen

1 Jamie: ....
2 Nicola: ....
3 Sam (their son): ....
4 Becky (their daughter): ....

6 ▶117 Listen again and complete the sentences from the conversation.

A phone call home
1 Oh, hi, Nicola. What are you **doing**?
2 I'm sitting in my hotel room and I'm .... on my laptop.
3 .... you cooking dinner?
4 I'm in the kitchen and I'm .... pasta.
5 And what's Sam doing? .... he watching TV?
6 Is he .... computer games?
7 No, he .... He's doing homework in the dining room.
8 And what about Becky? What's she ....?
9 Becky – what .... you doing?
10 .... friends, Dad. Oh, and I'm cleaning my bedroom.
11 She's messaging friends and .... cleaning her bedroom.

Out and about

7 Complete the grammar box with the correct verb forms.

Grammar: Present Continuous ▶ PAGE 95

Positive
We form the Present Continuous with the correct form of *be* + verb + *-ing*.
I **am working**.   He/she/it **is working**.
You/we/they ¹..................... .

Negative
We form the negative with the correct form of *be* + *not* + verb + *-ing*:
I'm not cooking dinner. / She ² .... dinner. / They **aren't cooking** dinner.

Questions and answers
Are you **working**? Yes, I ³..................... . / No, **I'm not**.
Is he **working**?   Yes, he **is**. / No, he ⁴..................... .
What ⁵..................... you **doing**?
I'm working on my laptop.
We use the Present Continuous for actions that are happening now.

8 Complete the conversations with the Present Continuous form of the verbs in brackets.

1 **A:** Hi, Daniel. __Are__ you __doing__ your maths homework? (*do*)
   B: No, I .... my homework. I .... dinner for my parents. (*not do / cook*)

2 **A:** You can't watch a film on TV because your dad .... a football match. (*watch*)
   B: He .... a football match, Mum – he .... the kitchen. (*not watch / clean*)

3 **A:** Look, that's my brother. He .... on the phone. (*talk*)
   B: Oh, yeah. And that's Ed next to him. He .... coffee. (*drink*)

4 **A:** .... your parents .... TV? (*watch*)
   B: No, they aren't. They .... (*work*)

9 ▶118 Listen and check. Then work with a partner and practise the conversations.

10 Work with a partner. Look at the picture. Take turns to ask and answer questions about the people.

What's Ed doing?

He's working on his laptop. What's Meg doing?

11 Work in small groups. Mime an action. Use the ideas in the box or your own ideas. Can the students in your group say what you are doing?

play computer games   read a book
cook dinner   talk on the phone   play the guitar
play golf

Are you playing computer games?

No, I'm not.

9B Now and usually

▶ **Grammar:** *Present Continuous and Present Simple*
▶ **Vocabulary:** *Holidays and activities*
▶ **Reading:** *A break from normal life*
▶ **Pronunciation:** *Word stress*

1 Work with a partner. Match the pictures to the types of holiday.

Type of holiday	Picture	Activities
1 city break		
2 skiing holiday		
3 countryside break		
4 beach holiday		

2 Which types of holiday do you sometimes go on? Where do you go? Tell your partner.

3 Look at the activities. Add them to the chart in exercise 1.

sightseeing

walking

skiing

cycling

shopping

swimming

snowboarding

sunbathing

4 Work with a partner. How do you say the words in the box? Underline the stress in each one. The first one is done for you.

> <u>coun</u>tryside   holiday   cycling   sightseeing
> skiing   sunbathing   snowboarding
> walking   shopping   swimming

5 ▶ 119 Listen, check and repeat.

6 What types of holiday do you like best? Put them in order from 1 (your favourite) to 4. Discuss your answers in small groups.

skiing holiday ....   beach holiday ....
countryside break ....   city break ....

> *Why do you like countryside breaks?*

> *Because I love walking. Why do you like …?*

7 ▶ 120 Read and listen to Sophie's blog, 'A break from normal life'. Answer the questions.
1 Where does Sophie usually live?
2 Where does she usually work?
3 What time does she usually start and finish work?
4 How does she usually travel to work?
5 Where is she living now?
6 Where is she working now?
7 What time is she starting and finishing work now?
8 How is she travelling to work now?

64

Out and about

A BREAK from *normal life*

My name is **Sophie** and I live in an apartment in London. I work for a design company. I usually start work at 8.30 and I sit at my desk until I finish at six. I travel to work by train – it takes 45 minutes! I like my job, but I don't like British winters, so …

… at the moment I am living in a beach hut in Goa, India. It's January and I have a month's holiday from my design job. So, I'm not sitting at my desk now! I'm sunbathing and swimming in the sea and then I have a job here. I'm working at my friend's beach bar. I'm starting work at five pm and I'm finishing at 1 am! And I'm not travelling by train every day. I'm walking to work – it takes five minutes! It's ten in the morning right now, and I'm drinking a smoothie at the beach bar and I'm writing this blog! I love it here!

8 Look at the blog again. Answer the questions.
1. What tense is underlined?
2. What tense is highlighted?

9 Complete the grammar box with the words in the box.

> now   don't   usually

Grammar: Present Simple and Present Continuous
▶ PAGE 95

We use the Present Simple for things that are true, or actions that happen ¹................... or every day:
*I live in an apartment in London. I **work** for a design company.*

We use the Present Continuous for things that are happening ²................... .
I'm drinking a smoothie at the beach bar. (= happening now)

We can also use the Present Continuous for things that are temporary (they ³................... happen usually).
I'm working at a beach bar in the evenings. (= temporary)

10 Look at Sophie's blog again. Underline examples of the Present Simple and circle examples of the Present Continuous.

11 Complete the conversations with the Present Simple or Present Continuous of the verbs in brackets. Then practise them with a partner.

1. **A:** Where are Jane and Richard today? They usually .... to this art class. (come)
   B: They're on holiday at the moment. They .... in Austria. (ski)
2. **A:** Where .... you usually .... on your summer holiday? (go)
   B: We usually .... to France. (go)
3. **A:** .... you .... in your own house? (live)
   B: No. I want to buy a house but I .... with my parents at the moment, until I have enough money. (live)
4. **A:** Hi, Greg. Where .... you ....? (go)
   B: I .... to the swimming pool. I always .... on Monday evenings. (go, swim)
5. **A:** Why isn't Dave at work?
   B: He's on holiday – he .... in the Pyrenees in Spain with his brother. (cycle)
6. **A:** What .... your sister .... at the moment? (do)
   B: She .... in America for four months. She .... at a skiing hotel in Colorado. (live, work)

12 Imagine you are living your perfect holiday life for one month. Complete the information about your normal life and your perfect holiday life.

NORMAL LIFE (usually)
Home:
Work/school:
Travel to work/school:
Start and finish times:
HOLIDAY LIFE (now)
Holiday home:
Holiday work/activities:
Activity right now:

13 Work with a partner. Take turns to talk about your normal life and your holiday life. Use the Present Simple and the Present Continuous.

> *Usually I …, but at the moment I'm …*

9C Meeting up

▶ **Speaking:** Meeting friends
▶ **Writing:** Social media posts

Speaking

1 Work in small groups. Discuss the questions.
   1 Where do you usually meet your friends?
   2 Are you often late for friends? Why? / Why not?
   3 Are your friends or colleagues often late? How do you feel about this?

2 ▶121 Listen to three conversations. Match them to pictures A–C.
   Conversation 1: ....
   Conversation 2: ....
   Conversation 3: ....

3 ▶121 Complete the *Key Language* box with the words in the box. Listen again and check.

| are | down | finishing | can | late | minutes |
| see | sitting | up | waiting | with | |

KEY LANGUAGE Meeting friends

Starting the call
(Jake), you're ^{1}............! Where ^{2}............ you?
You're 20 ^{3}............ late!

Saying where you are
We're/I'm ^{4}............ outside the office/entrance …
I'm running/driving ^{5}............ (London Road).
I'm ^{6}............ an email.
I'm ^{7}............ in the café …

Ending the call
I can be ^{8}............ you in one minute.
Hurry ^{9}............!
I ^{10}............ see you now.
^{11}............ you in a minute.

4 There is one word missing from each line of the sentences. Write the missing words.

Conversation 1
1 You're late!
2 Sorry. I running down York Street right now.
3 OK. I'm sitting the café waiting for you.
4 I be there in five minutes.
5 OK. up!

Conversation 2
6 Hi, Jo! Where you?
7 I driving down Main Road.
8 I'm waiting the cinema entrance.
9 I can there in one minute.
10 OK. See you in minute.

5 Work with a partner. Practise the conversations in exercise 4.

🌱 YOUR TURN

6 Work with a partner. Student A turn to page 101. Student B turn to page 105.

7 Work with a new partner. You are meeting a friend and you are late. Think of a reason. Have two phone conversations.

> Hi, Marco. Where are you?

> Hi, Maria. Sorry I'm late. I'm …

Out and about

Writing

1 Do the quiz. Discuss your answers in small groups.

Social media quiz
1. Which of these do you use? Why?
   Facebook □ YouTube □
   Instagram □ WeChat □ Twitter □
2. How many messages or photos do you post every week?
   0–3 □ 3–10 □ 11–20 □ more than 20 □
3. Do you think that some people post too often?
4. Why do you think they do this?

2 Complete the five posts on the right with the hashtags.

> #familylife #holidays #lovesport
> #saturdaynight #workinglate

3 Read the *Key Language* box. Complete it with the words in the box.

> amazing   be   Present Continuous

KEY LANGUAGE Social media posts

We often use verbs in the ¹............... in updates to say what we are doing: *I'm sitting at my desk ...*
In lists, we don't usually repeat the subject + ²...............
I'm sunbathing, reading, and listening to music.
~~I'm sunbathing, I'm reading, and I'm listening to music.~~
We often use adjectives in social media updates:
a **beautiful** swimming pool, an ³............... new dress, some **black** coffee, a **wonderful** garden, my **best** friend

4 Write the words in the correct order to make social media updates.
1. sitting on / strawberries. #lazyday / my blue sofa, reading / I'm / a book and eating
2. friend. #lovebikes / beautiful countryside with / I'm / my best / cycling in the
3. for our lunch. / We're / #lunchout / café, talking and waiting / drinking coffee in the new
4. #citybreak / waiting at the / to wonderful / New York. / airport for / We're / a plane

🡒 YOUR TURN

5 Work with a partner.
1. Write a social media update on a piece of paper. Use a hashtag. Give it to your partner.
2. Read your partner's update. Are there any mistakes?

6 Find a photo or take a selfie. Write an update in English for your photo or selfie. Send it to a friend.

♡ 💬 ✈   🔖
1 I'm sunbathing by this beautiful swimming pool, reading, and listening to music. ....

♡ 💬 ✈   🔖
2 I'm wearing my amazing new dress and dancing with friends. ....

♡ 💬 ✈   🔖
3 It's 11 pm. and I'm sitting at my desk, writing an article and drinking black coffee. ....

♡ 💬 ✈   🔖
4 I'm drinking coffee in my wonderful garden, reading a book, and watching my son play. ....

♡ 💬 ✈   🔖
5 I'm running with my best friend, talking and doing exercise at the same time. ....

10 Places

- **Vocabulary:** *Rooms*
- **Listening:** *Describing a holiday rental*
- **Grammar:** *There is / there are*

10A Holiday rentals

1. Work with a partner. Match the words in the box to the pictures.

   > bathroom   bedroom   dining room   garden
   > garage   hall   kitchen   living room   toilet

2. ▶123 Listen and check. Then listen again and repeat. Which of the rooms or places does your house or flat have?

3. Look at the three adverts for places to stay on holiday. Where you you usually look to find places to stay?

B

HOUSE WITH LARGE GARDEN
Cost: 1600 euros
8 guests · 4 bedrooms · 3 ³............... · kitchen ·
hall · living room · dining room · toilet ·
big garden · ⁴............... for car

A

MODERN APARTMENT
Cost: 1050 euros
¹............... guests · 3 ²............... ·
1 bathroom · kitchen · living room

C

HISTORIC FLAT
Cost: ⁵............... euros
6 guests · 3 bedrooms · 2 bathrooms · living room ·
kitchen with a ⁶............... · toilet · on-street
parking

Places

4 ▶124 Listen to Caroline and Ian talking about the three places to stay on holiday. Which one do they NOT choose?

5 ▶124 Listen again and complete the adverts with the correct words. Which place do you like? Why?

6 ▶125 Listen to their next conversation. Which place do they choose? Why?

7 Match the sentences to the three places in the adverts.
1 There are three bedrooms. ....
2 There's also a garage for the car. ....
3 There isn't a dining room, but there is a table in the kitchen. ....
4 There aren't any shops or restaurants near there. ....

8 ▶126 Listen and check.

9 Complete the grammar box with *is*, *isn't*, *are* and *aren't*.

> **Grammar: *There is / there are*** ▶ PAGE 96
>
> We use *there is* or *there are* to talk about things we can see or things that exist.
> **Positive** There ¹ *is* a garden. There ² .... three bedrooms.
> **Negative** There **isn't** a toilet. There ³ .... any restaurants.
> **Questions and answers**
> How many rooms ⁴ .... **there**? What furniture **is there**?
> ⁵ .... a garage? Yes, **there is**. / No, **there** ⁶ ....
> ⁷ .... **there** any shops? Yes, **there** ⁸ .... / No, **there aren't**.

10 Complete the conversations with the correct form of *there is* or *there are*.

1
A: .... a café near the flat?
B: Yes, ... And .... three restaurants too.

2
A: .... a garage?
B: No, ... , but .... a parking space for one car.

3
A: .... two bedrooms?
B: No .... one bedroom and a sofa bed in the living room.

4
A: .... any WiFi?
B: No, ... That's terrible! The kids need WiFi!

11 Write an advert for an amazing place to stay. Describe the number of rooms and the things to do nearby.

Cost ....
Rooms ....
Things to do nearby ....

12 Work in groups. Ask questions about each other's places to stay. Choose your favourite one.

> *Is there a balcony?*

> *No, there isn't, but there's a really big garden!*

10B Where were you?

> **Grammar:** Was / were
> **Vocabulary:** Places in a town; Prepositions
> **Listening:** Where were you last night?

1 ▶127 Match the pictures to the places in the box. Then listen and check.

> cinema   hospital   hotel   museum   restaurant
> school   station   supermarket   swimming pool

2 Work with a partner. Which places in exercise 1 are there in your town?

> *There are some hotels, but there isn't a museum.*

3 ▶128 Listen to five conversations. Where were the people last night? Match the people to the places.

Speaker 1	at home
Speaker 2	in London
Speaker 3	in a restaurant
Speaker 4	in the supermarket
Speaker 5	on a train

4 ▶128 Listen again. Write the correct number speaker for each answer.

                                            Speaker

1 Who enjoys shopping late at night? ......
2 Who was with friends? ......
3 Who was in bed at 11? ......
4 Who works late? ......
5 Who was with their husband? ......

5 Complete the table with *in*, *at* or *on*.

Preposition	Place
1	home, university, the station, a party
2	a taxi, the city centre, London, class, a restaurant, the park
3	holiday, the internet, the television, a bus, a train, a plane

Places

6 Complete the sentences with *in*, *at* or *on*.
1. I was .... the city centre last weekend.
2. I was .... university in 2020.
3. I was .... a party on Saturday night.
4. I was .... holiday in June last year.
5. I was .... the park on Sunday afternoon.
6. I was .... a bus this morning.

7 Tick the sentences in exercise 6 that are true for you. Change the other sentences to make them true for you. Tell a partner.

8 Look at the conversations. Complete the grammar box with the words in bold.

"Where were you last night?"
"I was in London."
"Were you with friends?"
"Yes, I was. We **were** at the cinema together."

"Where were you last night?"
"I was out with my husband. It was his birthday and we were in the new Greek restaurant in town."
"**Was** the restaurant good?"
"No, it **wasn't**. It was terrible!"

Grammar: Was / were ▶ PAGE 96

We use was or were to talk about the past. They are the Past Simple form of *be*.

Positive
I/he/she/it **was** at home.
You/we/they ¹.................. at home.

Negative
I/he/she/it ².................. at home.
You/we/they **weren't** at home.

Questions and answers
Where **were you** last night?
³.................. the film good? Yes, it ⁴................... No, it ⁵...................
⁶.................. they excited? Yes, they ⁷................... No, they **weren't**.

9 Choose the correct words to complete the sentences.
1. Where *were / was* you last weekend? *Was / Were* you with your family?
2. How *was / were* the restaurant on Friday night? *Was / were* it very busy?
3. *Were / Was* you in class on Tuesday? *Was / Were* there any homework?
4. How *was / were* your holiday? *Were / was* the kids excited in Disneyland?

10 Complete the answers with *was*, *wasn't*, *were* or *weren't*.
1. I .... with my family. We .... at an 80th birthday party for my grandmother. It .... a big party, only our family.
2. It .... busy, but I don't know why. It .... very good! The food .... OK, but the service .... very slow and it .... cheap!
3. I .... in the lesson, but don't worry, there .... any homework.
4. It .... great! We .... only in Disneyland for one day. It .... amazing for the kids. They .... really excited.

11 Work in pairs. Ask and answer the questions. Ask another question to get more information.

Where were you yesterday at 8:00 am?

Where were you yesterday at 10:00 am?

Where were you yesterday at 6:30 pm?

Where were you last night?

Where were you on Saturday?

Where were you on Sunday?

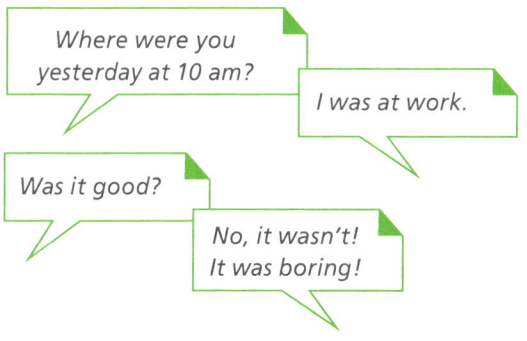

Where were you yesterday at 10 am?
I was at work.
Was it good?
No, it wasn't! It was boring!

10C A new place

▶ **Speaking:** Asking for and giving directions
▶ **Writing:** An email; Describing your home and where it is

Speaking

1 Look at the map. Label A–D with the words in the box.

> car park   park   school   train station

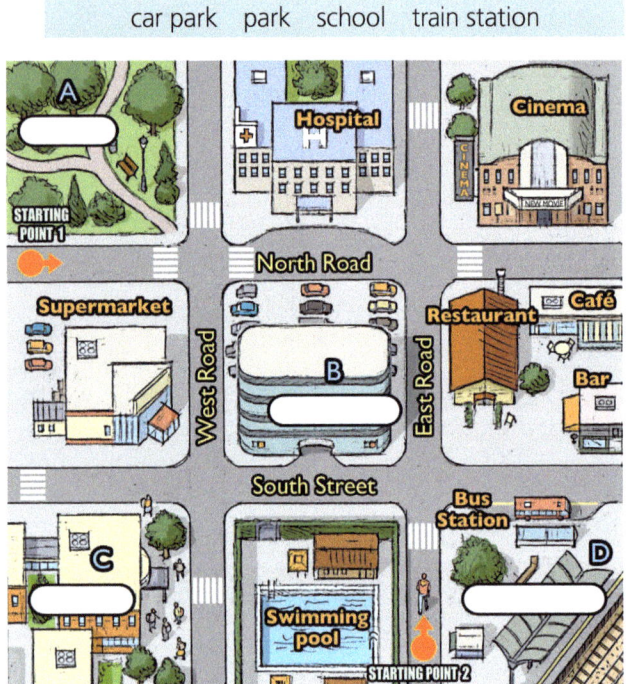

2 ▶129 Look at the pictures and the words. Then listen and complete the sentences with the correct words.

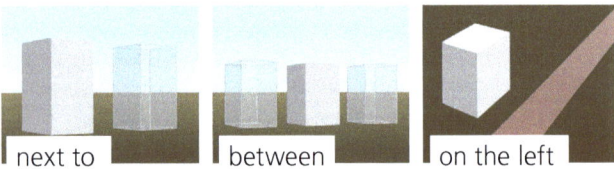
next to   between   on the left

opposite   on the corner   on the right

1 There's a café on North Road .... the Chinese restaurant and the Irish bar.
2 It's at the end of West Road, on the ....
3 There's a restaurant on the .... of East Road and North Road.
4 Yes, there's a car park on South Street, ... the swimming pool.
5 There's a park at the end of East Road, on the ....
6 The bus station is on South Street, ... the train station.

3 ▶130 Match the words in the box to the pictures. Listen and check.

> turn left   turn right   go straight on

4 ▶131 Look at the person at Starting point 2 on the map in exercise 1. Listen to the directions. Mark where the cash machine is.

5 Complete the phrases in the *Key Language* box with the words in the box.

> corner   go   near   on   is   to

KEY LANGUAGE Asking for and giving directions

Asking for directions
Is there a café ¹................... here?
Excuse me. Where ²................... the hospital?

Saying where something is
It's ³................... the right / left.
It's next ⁴................... the station.
It's between the Chinese restaurant and the Irish bar.
It's on the ⁵................... .
It's opposite the cinema.

Giving directions
Turn left / right at the end of the road.
⁶................... straight on.

YOUR TURN

6 Work with a partner. Find starting point 1 and starting point 2 on the map and have two conversations.

Starting point 1: Student A, ask Student B for directions to the train station.

Starting point 2: Student B, ask Student A for directions to the hospital.

7 Look at the map again with your partner and take turns.
1 Choose a starting point and a finishing point.
2 Tell your partner the starting point but NOT the finishing point.
3 Give directions to the finishing point.
4 Did your partner find the correct finishing point?

Places

Writing

1 Work in small groups. Where do you live? What do you like about your home? What do you like about the place where your home is?

2 Read the email. What does Vicky love about her new flat?

Hi Sam,
How are you? I'm in my new flat now! It's really nice. It's very clean and modern. The flat is on the fourth floor and I can see the park from the balcony.
The flat is quite big. There's a kitchen, a living room, a bathroom and two bedrooms. I really love the kitchen. There's a small balcony next to the kitchen and I often have a coffee there in the morning or a glass of wine in the evening.
I love the location of my flat – I can walk in the park and I can cycle to work. There are lots of buses and trains nearby. The nightlife is good and there are lots of things to do. There are some cafés, bars and shops on the high street near my flat. It's a five-minute walk, so it's really near.
I love it here! Please come and visit. I have two bedrooms! 😊
Love,
Vicky

3 Read the email again and answer the questions.
1 What floor is her flat on?
2 What rooms are there in Vicky's flat?
3 What is next to the kitchen?
4 What does she like doing on the balcony?
5 How does she get to work?
6 What things are near her flat?
7 Where can her friend sleep?

4 Read the *Key Language* box. Complete it with words from the email.

KEY LANGUAGE Describing where you live

It's very clean / nice / ¹........................... .
I can ² .... the park from the balcony.
The flat is on the first / second / third / ³ ....
I can ⁴ .... in the park.
There are lots of ⁵ .... and trains.
There are some cafés, bars and shops on the high street ⁶........................... my flat.
It's a five-minute ⁷..........................., so it's really near.

5 Complete some more sentences for describing where you live. Use the words in the box.

| aren't   aren't very good   beautiful   car |
| ground   the river   thirty-minute |

1 My flat is old and really ....
2 The flat is on the .... floor.
3 I can see .... from my balcony.
4 The buses and trains ....
5 The best way to get around is by ....
6 There .... any shops near my house.
7 It's a .... walk to the station.

YOUR TURN

6 Write an email to a friend.
- Describe your house or flat and where it is.
- Say what you like and don't like about it.
- Use the *Key Language* box to help you.

Video 5: Hotels and holidays

5 Hotels and holidays

1 Work with a partner. Discuss the questions.
   1 Where do you like going on holiday? Why?
   2 What activities do you like doing on holiday?
   3 Where do you usually stay on holiday? Do you camp or stay in a hotel or apartment?

2 Read about two hotels. Where is the Tree House hotel? Where is the Salt hotel?

3 Read the article again. Answer the questions.
   1 Which two places do tourists like going to in Costa Rica?
   2 Why are the tree house hotels great places to stay?
   3 How big is the salt flat in Bolivia?
   4 What is different about the walls, tables and chairs in the salt hotel?

4 Work with a partner. Which hotel from the article would you like to visit? Why?

Two unusual places to stay

There are lots of interesting places to visit around the world and some of the hotels are very unusual!

TREE HOUSE HOTEL

There are lots of things to see and do in Costa Rica. The beaches are beautiful and there is also a big rainforest. People like seeing all the different animals and plants in the rainforest. There are lots of tree house hotels in the rainforest. They are great places to stay because you have amazing views of the rainforest from your bedroom window.

SALT HOTEL

In Bolivia there is a place called Salar de Uyuni. It is a large area of land (10,582 square kilometres) that is covered in salt. Lots of tourists come to visit each year. The local people build houses and hotels from the salt, so you can stay in a salt hotel! In these hotels, the walls are salt and so are the tables and chairs! There are also beautiful views of the salt flat from each bedroom.

5 Watch the video. Tick ✓ the places you hear about.
1 Iceland ....
2 Norway ....
3 Indian Ocean ....
4 Los Angeles ....
5 Barcelona ....
6 New Orleans ....
7 New York ....

6 Watch the video again. Answer the questions.
1 Where is the ice hotel?
2 Where is the underwater hotel?
3 Which city has buildings by Antoni Gaudí?
4 What are two usual places to visit in New York?
5 How high above the street is the High Line park?
6 What was the High Line before it was a park?

7 Work in small groups. Discuss the questions.
1 Which place in the video would you like to visit? Why?
2 Do many tourists visit your country? Where do they usually go?

Review

LESSON 9A	What verbs do we use with *homework*, *dinner* and *selfies*?
LESSON 9A	What are you doing right now? Write two sentence in the Present Continuous.
LESSON 9B	Write 4 holiday activities.
LESSON 9B	Complete this sentence about you: *I usually* ...., *but at the moment I* ....
LESSON 9C	You are late to meet a friend. Write a sentence to say why.
LESSON 9C	Write an Instagram post about what you're doing today.
LESSON 10A	Write all the rooms in your house or apartment.
LESSON 10A	Write sentences about the room you are in. Use *there is* and *there are*.
LESSON 10B	Where were you yesterday? Where were your friends? Write 2 sentences using *was* and *were*.
LESSON 10B	Do we use *on*, *in* or *at* with these words: *home*, *Madrid*, *holiday*?
LESSON 10C	Write directions from your home to the nearest supermarket.
LESSON 10C	Write 3 sentences to describe your house or apartment.

75

11 Last week

- **Vocabulary:** *Phrases with do, go, get and have*
- **Listening:** *What did you do yesterday?*
- **Grammar:** *Past Simple: Common irregular verbs*

11A Last weekend

1 Choose the correct words to complete the phrases in the sentences.
1. I usually *get / go up* at seven o'clock and *have / do a shower*.
2. I always *do / get my homework* before *I go / have dinner*.
3. I *get / do sport* or *go / do to the gym* every day.
4. I never *do / have a coffee* before I *go / do to bed*.
5. I sometimes *have / go for a run* before I *go / do to work*.
6. At the weekend, I *have / go shopping* and *have / do a good time* with my friends.
7. I usually *do / go the housework* when I *get / do home* from work.

2 Change four of the sentences in exercise 1 so they are true for you. Compare with a partner.

3 ▶133 Listen to Sarah and Mark talking about last Sunday. Tick the things Mark did.

> do sport   do the housework
> do your homework   get up
> go shopping   go to the gym
> have a coffee   have a shower

4 Underline the Past Simple forms of *have*, *go*, *get* and *do*.
1. I got up at ten o'clock.
2. We had a coffee in a café.
3. We went shopping in the city centre.
4. In the evening, I did some housework.

5 Complete the grammar box with *got* and *went*.

Grammar: Past Simple: Common irregular verbs
▶ PAGE 106

A lot of common verbs are irregular in the Past Simple.
I **go** shopping every day. Yesterday I ¹ .... shopping.
I usually **get** up at seven o'clock. Yesterday, I ² .... up at six.
The Past Simple form is the same for all subjects.
I you/he/we/they ³ .... shopping yesterday.
See page 106 for a list of common irregular verbs.

6 Read about Sarah's day yesterday. Complete the sentences with the past simple of *do*, *go*, *get* and *have*.
1. Yesterday was a busy day. I .... up at 6 am!
2. There was no time for breakfast, so I just .... a coffee.
3. I .... a lot of sport! I .... for a run at 7 am.
4. Then I .... to the gym!
5. I had a lot of work to do, so I .... to my office on Sunday afternoon!
6. I .... home at 8 pm!

7 ▶133 Listen to Sarah and Mark again. Complete the sentences with *did* or *didn't*.
1. What .... you do on Sunday?
2. '............ you buy any new clothes?' 'Yes, I ....'
3. .... you do anything interesting in the evening?
4. No, I .... I usually do sport on Sunday evenings, but I .... do any sport yesterday.

Last week

8 Complete the grammar box with the correct words.

> **Grammar: Past Simple: negatives and questions** ▶ PAGE 96
>
> **Negative**
> We use ¹.................. + verb. The form doesn't change.
> I **didn't go** to work yesterday. We **didn't have** lunch.
>
> **Questions and answers**
> We use ².................. + subject + verb to make questions.
> What time **did** you get up?
> **Did** you get up early? Yes, I **did**. / No, I ³.................. .

9 Write questions in the Past Simple.
1 you / have a meal in a restaurant last weekend?
   Did you have a meal in a restaurant last weekend?
2 you / go out for a drink last night?
3 you / get up early this morning?
4 you / go to a party last month?
5 you / have a shower this morning?
6 you / have a good day yesterday?

10 Complete the answers with the negative form of the words in brackets. Match the answers to the questions in exercise 9.
1 No, I .... (have) a good day. It was a terrible day!
2 No, I .... (go out) for a drink. I stayed at home.
3 No, I .... (have) a meal in a restaurant. I went to a friend's house for dinner.
4 No, I .... (have) a shower this morning. I had one last night.
5 No, I .... (go) to a party last month, but I went to my brother's party in April.
6 No, I .... (get) up early this morning. I don't work on Fridays.

11 Work with a partner. Ask and answer the questions in exercise 9.

> Did you have a meal in a restaurant last weekend?

> Yes, I did. I went to an Italian restaurant with my wife.

12 Work in pairs. Read the questions. Then complete the answers with the irregular Past Simple forms in the box.

> ate   bought   caught   came   drank
> left   met   saw   slept   ~~woke~~

1 **A:** What time did you <u>wake</u> up this morning?
   B: I _woke_ up at 7:30.
2 **A:** When did you last <u>catch</u> a train?
   B: I .... a train at the weekend.
3 **A:** How many coffees did you <u>drink</u> this morning?
   B: I .... four coffees this morning.
4 **A:** Did you <u>see</u> your friends on Saturday?
   B: Yes, I did. I .... Paul at a football match.
5 **A:** When did you last <u>buy</u> a present for someone?
   B: I .... a new dress for my sister, for her birthday.
6 **A:** Did your parents <u>come</u> to your flat this weekend?
   B: Yes, they did. They .... for dinner on Saturday night.
7 **A:** What did you <u>eat</u> for breakfast this morning?
   B: I .... some toast and cereal.
8 **A:** When did you <u>leave</u> home this morning?
   B: I .... at 8:30.
9 **A:** How long did you <u>sleep</u> last night?
   B: I .... for eight hours.

13 ▶134 Listen and check.

14 Work with a partner. Ask and answer the questions in exercise 12.

15 Take turns. Use the verbs to ask your partner questions about last weekend.

> buy   catch   come   do   drink   eat   get
> go   have   leave   see   meet   speak

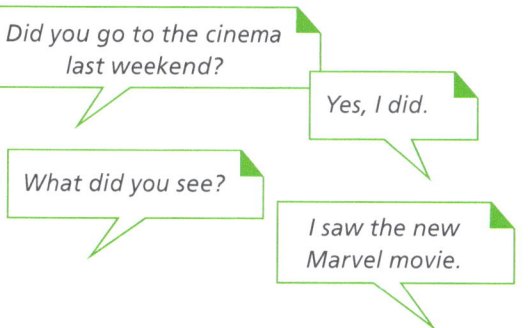

11B My best experience

- Grammar: *Past Simple: Regular verbs*
- Vocabulary: *Adjectives to describe experiences*
- Pronunciation: *Past Simple endings*
- Reading: *My experiences abroad*
- Listening: *My best experiences*

1 Read the three blog posts. Match the people to the places in the pictures.

A

B

Susie

I arrived in Japan a week before my course started. So, I went on holiday and visited Kyoto and Osaka. My university was in Tokyo. Tokyo is a huge city and I took the train every day. I hated the train. It was so <u>crowded</u>! But I loved everything else about my time in Japan. I met new friends from all over the world. The food was <u>excellent</u>! I love Sushi. Lots of people think Japan is expensive but the sushi was really cheap. I really enjoyed the summer fireworks festival. Some families waited all day on the streets to get one of the best places!

Nicki

I finished my year abroad last month. I liked living in California. It was one of the best experiences in my life! At first, it was <u>difficult</u>. I didn't know anyone and everything was new. The first two weeks I stayed in a hotel. It was really <u>boring</u> on my own! Then, I lived with a really kind family. They were really funny – I laughed a lot and they cooked some amazing food! After two weeks, a student in my class invited me to a party. Everyone was really <u>friendly</u>. I talked to so many people. We danced and had fun for hours! I didn't want to leave 🙁 I met so many friends. I stopped feeling bored and had fun.

Tim

In the UK I studied English Literature at university, but in Sydney I studied very <u>different</u> subjects. I learned about history, politics and business. It was really <u>interesting</u> and new. The university is very international. I met people from all over the world. I also helped in some of the English classes for international students. Now I am back in the UK and I am taking a course to become a teacher of English. I want to travel and teach around the world!

C

2 Read the blogs again and answer the questions.
1 Where did Susie go on holiday?
2 What did she hate in Tokyo?
3 What didn't cost much in Japan?
4 Where did Nicki stay at first in California?
5 Did she like the family she lived with?
6 Where did she meet lots of friends?
7 What subjects did Tim study in Australia?
8 Who did Tim help?
9 What is he doing now?

3 Match the underlined adjectives in the blogs to the meanings.
1 very good ....
2 not interesting ....
3 not easy ....
4 full, with lots of people ....
5 kind and nice to other people ....
6 unusual or not the same ....
7 exciting to learn about ....

4 Work with a partner. Talk about:
- something boring you did recently.
- an interesting TV programme you saw.
- someone you know who is friendly.
- an excellent meal you had.
- something difficult you did last week.

> Work was boring last week. I didn't have a lot to do

> I saw an interesting programme on TV last night. It was about …

Last week

5 ▶ 135 Listen to two American friends talking about their best experiences on a year abroad. Match the places and activities to the people.

Florence .... Rochelle ....

6 ▶ 135 Listen again and answer the questions.
1. When did Florence study Mandarin?
2. What did she do in the afternoon?
3. What were her favourite cities?
4. How long did she stay in China?
5. What problems did Rochelle have with people's accents in Liverpool?
6. What happened when Rochelle tried to cook?
7. Who cooked for Rochelle?

7 Look at the sentences and questions from the conversation. Complete the grammar box with the underlined words and letters.
1. Where <u>did</u> you stay?
2. I stay<u>ed</u> in Suzhou.
3. We <u>didn't</u> work.

Grammar: Past Simple: Regular verbs ▶ PAGE 97

Positive
For regular verbs, we add ¹.................: start**ed** stay**ed**

Spelling
Most verbs: + -ed work -> work**ed**, visit -> visit**ed**
Verbs ending in -e: + -d: love -> love**d**, like -> like**d**
Some verbs ending in -y: -> -ied: study -> stud**ied**
Some verbs double the final consonant: stop -> stop**ped**

Negatives and questions
In negatives, we use ²................. + verb: *I **didn't** want to leave.*
In questions, we use ³................. + subject + verb: *Where **did** you **live**?*
Did you have a good time? Yes, I did. / No, I didn't.

8 ▶ 136 Listen and repeat the verbs.

/d/	/t/	/ɪd/
closed	cooked	invited

9 ▶ 137 Add the verbs in the box to the table in exercise 8. Listen, check and repeat.

> asked   cleaned   enjoyed   finished   liked
> needed   started   talked   walked   wanted

10 ▶ 138 Complete the conversation with the Past Simple form of the verbs in brackets. Listen and check.

A: Where ¹ <u>did you go</u> (you / go) on holiday?
B: I ² .... (travel) around Europe for three weeks.
A: That sounds fun! Which place ³ .... (you / like) the most?
B: I ⁴ .... (love) Italy. We ⁵ .... (stay) there for a week. We ⁶ .... (visit) Venice and Rome.
A: I went to Rome last year. I really ⁷ .... (enjoy) it. Did you speak Italian when you were there?
B: I ⁸ .... (try). I ⁹ .... (ask) for directions one day, but I didn't understand the answer!
A: Ha! I was the same. ¹⁰ .... (you / like) Venice?
B: It was very beautiful, but I ¹¹ .... (not like) the weather. It ¹² .... (rain) for two days!

11 Work with a partner. Ask and answer questions about the topics in the boxes.

This morning:
listen to the radio   walk to school / work
talk to a friend / family member

Last night:
watch a movie   finish work late   cook dinner

Last weekend:
invite a friend out   clean your flat
help friends / family

> Did you listen to the radio this morning?

> Yes, I did. I listened to the radio in my car.

79

11C What was it like?

- **Speaking:** Giving opinions
- **Pronunciation:** Showing feelings
- **Writing:** A restaurant review; Describing your experience

Speaking

1 Work with a partner. When did you last do the activities in the pictures?

2 ▶139 Listen to four people talking about last weekend. What did they do? Match each person to an activity in exercise 1.
1 Sam ....
2 Beth ....
3 Nicki ....
4 Paul ....

3 ▶139 Listen again and answer the questions.
1 What did Sam think of the film?
2 Where did Beth eat out?
3 What was good about the restaurant?
4 Did Nicki enjoy Mark's band?
5 What did Mark do that wasn't very good?
6 Whose birthday party did Paul go to?
7 What is Paul doing on Thursday?

4 Complete the phrases in the *Key language* box with the words in the box.

> awful   boring   fantastic   great   like
> interesting   it   not very good   OK   time   was

> **KEY LANGUAGE** Giving opinions
>
> How ¹.................. it?
> What was it ².................. ?
> Did you enjoy ³.................. ?
> Did you have a good ⁴.................. ?
>
> **Positive adjectives:**
> It was … delicious / ⁵.......... / .... / ....
>
> **Negative adjectives:**
> It was … terrible / ⁶.......... / .... / ....
>
> **Neutral adjectives:**
> It was … all right / ⁷..........

5 ▶140 Listen to the sentences. Notice how the voice goes up for positive feelings and down for negative feelings. Then repeat and practise.
1 It was delicious!   3 It was terrible!
2 It was amazing!   4 It was boring!

6 Work with a partner. Ask and answer questions about things in the box. Use phrases and adjectives from the *Key Language* box. Remember to use the correct intonation.

YOUR TURN

7 Make notes about the last time you went to a party, a restaurant, the cinema or a concert. Answer the questions.
- Where did you go?
- What did you eat, see or do?
- What was it like?

8 Work with a partner. Ask and answer questions about the events you went to.

Writing

1 Work with a partner. Think of the last restaurant you went to. Give it a score for each thing. Compare with a partner and explain your scores.

Where did you go?

How was the food?

2 Work with a partner. Read Emma's review. What score do you think Emma gave the restaurant for each category? Why?

> We ate here on Saturday night. It is a family-friendly restaurant and we went with our two children. The restaurant is on a lovely street in the old town. It's a really beautiful building and great place. To start with, I ate a tomato salad. For my main course I had fish in a tomato sauce and for dessert I had a chocolate brownie. The food was good, but very expensive. The waiter was really friendly, but the service was a bit slow. I would probably come here again but mainly because of where it is and because it is a beautiful building.
>
> **(Emma)**

3 Answer the questions.
1. When did Emma eat in the restaurant?
2. Where is the restaurant?
3. What did Emma eat for her main course?
4. What did Emma eat for dessert?
5. Was it a cheap meal?
6. What was the problem with the service?

4 Read the *Key Language* box. Complete it with words from Emma's review.

KEY LANGUAGE Describing your experience

Describing the food you ate
To start ¹……………………, I ate …
For my main course/dessert I ²…………………… …

Describing the restaurant and the location
It is a family-³…………………… restaurant.
The restaurant is ⁴…………………… a lovely street.

Giving your opinion on the food and service
The food was amazing/terrible/OK/ ⁵…………………….
The ⁶…………………… was (really/very) friendly.
The service was (a bit/very) ⁷…………………….
The meal was good, ⁸…………………… very expensive.
The food was really good value.

Recommending
I would probably/definitely come here ⁹…………………… .
I wouldn't recommend this restaurant.

5 Complete the sentences with the correct words.

> ate   awful   centre   definitely   modern
> value   wasn't   wouldn't

1. To start with, I …………………… a salad.
2. The restaurant is in a …………………… building.
3. The restaurant is in the town …………………… .
4. The food was ……………………!
5. The waiter …………………… very friendly.
6. The food was really good …………………… .
7. I …………………… come here again.
8. I would …………………… come here again.

🌱 YOUR TURN

6 Think about the last time you ate out. Write a review of the restaurant for a website. Write about:

- the food
- the location
- the service
- the price

12 Plans & experiences

- **Vocabulary:** *Phrases with do, get, go and move*
- **Grammar:** *Be going to*
- **Pronunciation:** *Weak form of 'to'*
- **Listening:** *A radio advert*
- **Reading:** *What next?*

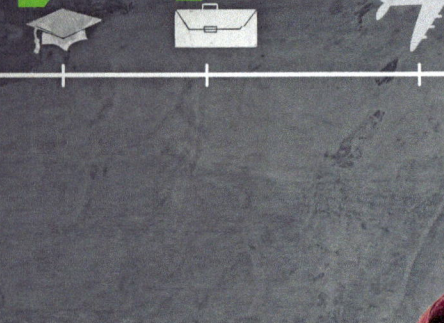

12A Future plans

WHAT NEXT?

My name's Simon and I'm 23. Last year I was a student, but university is finished now. Here's what five of my friends and I want to do next.

Ellie and Rob They're going to get jobs in London. Then they're going to buy an apartment and they're going to get married!

Isabel She isn't going to get a job. She's going to go travelling. She's going to visit India first and she's going to study yoga there.

Becky She's going to go to another university! She's going to do a masters degree in philosophy at Stanford, in the US.

Rick He's going to move to Los Angeles. He wants to be an actor, so he's going to do a drama course in the day and he's going to work in a restaurant in the evenings.

Simon (me) So, what about me? What am I going to do? Well, I'm going to move in with my sister – she lives in Manchester. And I'm going to start my own business.

1 Work with a partner. The man in the picture is thinking about his future.
  1 Match the words in the box to the five small pictures in the photo.

  > children   home   job   travelling   university

  2 At what age do people usually do these things in your country?

2 ▶143 Listen to an advert. Choose the correct answers.
  1 The journalist wants people to tell him about their *past experiences / plans for the future*.
  2 He wants people to *call / email* him.

3 ▶143 Complete the phrases with the words in the box. Listen again and check.

  > to university   married   a degree
  > in with (some friends)

do	a course	1 ....
get	a job	2 ....
go	travelling	3 ....
move	to London	4 ....

4 Work with a partner. Which activities in exercise 3 do you want to do:
  1 next month?
  2 next year?
  3 in the next five / ten years?

  > *I want to do a Russian course next month. What about you?*

  > *I want to move to Barcelona.*

5 ▶144 Simon sent an article to Josh about his friends. Read and listen to the article. Answer the questions. Who is going to …
  1 live with his sister? ....
  2 live in London? ....
  3 learn to act? ....
  4 go to Asia? ....
  5 study philosophy? ....

Plans & experiences

6 Read the article again. It's six months later. Match the people to the pictures of them now.

1 .... 2 ....

3 ....

4 .... 5 ....

7 Look at the underlined verb forms in Simon's article. Read the grammar box and choose the correct words to complete the rules.

Grammar: Be going to ▶ PAGE 97

We use be + going to + verb to talk about ¹past plans / now / future plans.

Positive
I'**m going to start** a business. She'**s going to go** travelling. They'**re going to buy** an apartment.

Negative
I'**m not going to start** a business. She **isn't going to go** travelling. They **aren't going to buy** an apartment.

Questions
For questions, the word order is ²the same as / different from the word order in positive sentences.

What **am** I **going to do**?   Where **is** she **going to live**?

8 ▶145 Complete the conversations with the correct form of be going to and the verbs in brackets. Then listen and check.

A: What ¹ <u>are</u> you <u>going to do</u> after university? (do)
B: I ² .... travelling in Australia. (go)
A: What ³ .... you .... there? (do)
B: I ⁴ .... a job in a hotel, but I ⁵ .... all the time. I ⁶ .... a surfing course, too. (get, not work, do)

A: What ⁷ .... you .... next year? (do)
B: I ⁸ .... a house. (buy)
A: Where ⁹ .... you .... it? (buy)
B: In Glasgow – so I ¹⁰ .... to Scotland. (move)
A: Why ¹¹ .... you .... there? (move)
B: My brother lives there. We ¹² .... together and he ¹³ .... me start my own business. (work, help)

9 ▶146 Listen to part of the first conversation again. Notice how the people say 'to' with a weak pronunciation. Listen again and repeat.

A: What are you going **to** do after university?
B: I'm going **to** go travelling in Australia.

10 Work with a partner. Practise the conversations in exercise 8.

11 Answer the questions in the table about you.

FUTURE PLANS

What are you going to do …?	You	S1	S2	S3
at the weekend				
next week				
next year				
in the next five/ten years				

12 Talk to other students. Ask and answer questions about future plans using be going to. Write about three other students in your table.

What are you going to do at the weekend?
I'm going to go shopping.
What are you going to buy?

13 Tell the class which students are similar to you.

83

12B Weekends

> Grammar: *Tense review*
> Vocabulary: *Adjectives to describe feelings*
> Reading: *Living for the weekend*

1 Underline the things you like doing at the weekend. Add other things that you like doing.

Where: stay at home / go to another city / go to another country
Money: buy new clothes / buy new books / buy nice food / buy nothing
Activities: do sport / read / watch TV / study / cook / go shopping / eat in a restaurant / visit museums
Socializing: meet friends / meet family / meet new people / meet nobody
Other things:

2 Work in small groups. Talk about your answers to exercise 1. Do you all like doing the same things at the weekend?

3 Read part 1 of the article 'Living for the weekend'. Complete it with the verbs in the box.

> am learning   am training   do   ~~get up~~   go   have   meet

4 Read part 2 of the article. Complete it with the Past Simple form of the verbs in brackets.

5 Read part 3 of the article. Complete it with *be going to* and the verbs in the box.

> be   drive   ~~go~~   see   stay

6 ▶ 147 Listen to the article. Check your answers to exercises 3, 4 and 5. Which exercise was the most difficult for you?

LIVING for the weekend!

We spoke to businessman, RALPH PACKER, about his weekends.

1 What do you usually do at weekends?

On Saturdays I ¹ *get up* late. I eat breakfast and I ² _____ my Spanish homework – I ³ _____ Spanish for work right now. After that I go to the gym or I run 15 km – I ⁴ _____ for a marathon at the moment. Then I ⁵ _____ a shower and I ⁶ _____ friends for dinner. On Sundays I often ⁷ _____ shopping or to the cinema.

2 What did you do last weekend?

Last weekend ¹ *was* (be) different. I ² _____ (go) to Iceland with my best friend. We ³ _____ (fly) to Reykjavik and then we ⁴ _____ (drive) north to Stykkisholmur, a beautiful fishing town. We ⁵ _____ (stay) there for three nights. We ⁶ _____ (visit) the volcano museum and we ⁷ _____ (walk) up a mountain. And we ⁸ _____ (see) the Northern Lights. It ⁹ _____ (be) an amazing weekend.

3 What are you going to do next weekend?

I'm really excited because I ¹ *'m going to go* to my brother's wedding! The wedding is in London, so I ² _____ there after work on Friday. And I ³ _____ in a hotel for two nights. It ⁴ _____ so much fun – I ⁵ _____ a lot of friends and family.

7 Look at the article again. Underline the correct answers.
1 What is Ralph studying at the moment? *Spanish / running*
2 When does he often go shopping? *on Saturdays / on Sundays*
3 Where did he stay for three nights? *Reykjavik / Stykkisholmur*
4 What did he walk up? *a mountain / a volcano*
5 When is his brother going to get married? *next Friday / next Saturday*
6 Where is Ralph going to stay? *at his brother's house / in a hotel*

Plans & experiences

8 Which part in the article talks about …
a the future? ....
b what usually happens? ....
c the past? ....
d what is happening now or around now? ....

9 Read the grammar box. Complete the rules with the tenses in the box.

be going to   Past Simple   Present Continuous
Present Simple

Grammar: tense review   ▶ PAGE 97

We use the ¹............ to talk about facts and routines (things that usually happen).

*On Saturdays I **get** up late.*

We use the ²............ to talk about things happening now or around now.

*I**'m training** for a marathon at the moment.*

We use the ³............ to talk about completed actions in the past.

*We **saw** the Northern Lights.*

We use ⁴............ to talk about future plans.

*He**'s going to get** married next Saturday.*

10 The bold verbs in the sentences are not correct. Write the correct sentences.
1 I **live** in Berlin in 2012. *I lived in Berlin in 2012.*
2 I **am often going** to the library after school.
   ....
3 I **going to start** a new job next week.
   ....
4 I **cook** dinner at the moment – can I call you back?
   ....
5 When **are you going to getting** married?
   ....
6 I can't speak now, I **drive**.
   ....
7 I **go** to Iceland on holiday last month.
   ....
8 Yesterday I **visit** the Tate Art gallery in London.
   ....

11 Match the messages to the emojis. Use the underlined adjectives to help you.

1 I didn't do anything last weekend. I stayed at home and watched TV. I was so <u>bored</u>.

2 We're flying to Delhi right now and we're going to travel round India for a month! I'm so <u>excited</u>!

3 I'm going to leave university next week. I'm going to be <u>sad</u> when I say goodbye to my friends.

4 We're walking up a big mountain. I'm really <u>tired</u> and there's a long way to walk!

5 I live in a beautiful country, I have a great job and wonderful friends. I'm very <u>happy</u>!

6 I opened my business last week. I spent a lot of money. I'm a bit <u>worried</u>!

a    b   c

d    e   f

12 ▶ 148 Listen and check. Then repeat and practise the adjectives.

13 Choose adjectives from exercise 11 to describe how you feel today. Tell a partner and give reasons.

I'm tired today.   *Why?*

Because I didn't sleep well last night.

14 Read the questions and think about your answers. Make notes. Think about which tense to use and use adjectives from exercise 11.
1 What do you usually do at the weekend?
2 What did you do last weekend? How did you feel?
3 What are you going to do next weekend? How do you feel about your plans?

15 Work in small groups. Ask and answer the questions in exercise 14. Who has similar answers?

12C Goodbye and thank you

▶ **Speaking:** Starting and ending a conversation
▶ **Writing:** Messages; Looking back and looking forwards

Speaking

1 Work with a partner. Read the article 'How to end a conversation'. Do you have the same rules in your language?

How to end a conversation

You're late for a meeting. You see a friend. The friends says hello and wants to talk. How do you end the conversation? Do you say: "Sorry, I can't talk now. Bye."?

NO! The best thing to do is …

- say something positive or nice.
- say why you are finishing the conversation.
- make a future plan.

So, for example:

"It's really good to see you, Mark. Sorry, but I'm late for a meeting. Let's meet up soon."

2 Read the example greeting at the end of the article. Find the sentence that …
　1　says something positive or nice.
　　　..
　2　says why the person is finishing the conversation.
　　　..
　3　makes a future plan. ....

3 ▶149 Listen to two conversations. Are the sentences True or False?
　1　Jeff doesn't know Kelly.
　2　Ed is meeting Jeff for the first time.
　3　Lisa and Noah are friends.
　4　Lisa is going to go to the gym.

4 ▶149 Choose the correct words to complete the sentences. Listen again and check.

1　Oh, is that *very late / the time*?
2　It was *really nice / OK* to meet you, Ed.
3　I *hope / want* we meet again. Bye.

4　Well, it was great to *see / meet* you.
5　Let's meet *up / with* soon.
6　*Message / Messaging* me.

5 Complete the phrases in the *Key Language* box with words from exercise 4.

KEY LANGUAGE Starting and ending a conversation

Saying hello
Hey, Lisa. / Hi, Noah. / Hello, Jeff.

Ending a conversation
Is that ¹..................?
It was really ².................. to meet you.
Well, it was ³.................. to see you.

Saying goodbye
See you later. / See you. / Bye.

Talking about future meetings
I hope we ⁴.................. again. Let's ⁵.................. soon.
Message ⁶...................

6 Match 1–5 with the answers a–e. Then practise with a partner.
　1　Nice to meet you, Marco.
　2　It was great to see you.
　3　How are you?
　4　Oh, is that the time? I'm late for my dinner date.
　5　Hey, Maria!

　a　I'm good, thanks.
　b　Yeah. Let's meet up soon.
　c　Oh, hi Luca!
　d　Oh, OK. See you later.
　e　Nice to meet you, too.

🔄 YOUR TURN

7 Work with a partner. Student A turn to page 101. Student B turn to page 105.

8 Stand up, walk around the class and speak to other students. In each conversation:
- say hello
- ask how he/she is
- end the conversation
- make a future plan
- say goodbye

Plans & experiences

Writing

1. Work with a partner. Look at the two pictures. Answer the questions.
   1. Which activities can you see in the pictures?

      a wedding   a party   a meeting   a dinner party

   2. Do you like cooking for friends?
   3. Talk about the last party you went to.

2. Read the messages and answer the questions.
   1. Who cooked dinner?
   2. Who had a party?
   3. Who is going to cook on Saturday?
   4. Whose birthday is next month?

 JANE: What a great party! Thanks for inviting us. It was great to see everybody.

 LUKE: It was so much fun! Thanks for coming. Let's meet up again soon.

 JANE: Yes, good idea. Let's go out to a restaurant for my birthday next month.

 LUKE: That sounds great!

 JOE: Thanks for a lovely dinner. It was great to see you.

 ELA: Thanks for coming! Let's do this again soon.

 JOE: Yes, good idea. Come to our house for dinner. When are you free next?

 ELA: We're free next Saturday.

 JOE: Great! See you next Saturday!

3. Complete the Key Language box with the words in the box. Use the messages in exercise 2 to help you.

   again   come   for   great   inviting   let's
   next   see   sounds   what   was

   ### KEY LANGUAGE Looking back and looking forwards
   Talking about a past activity
   Thanks ¹_____ a lovely dinner.
   ²_____ a great party!
   It ³_____ so much fun!
   Thanks for ⁴_____ us. / Thanks for coming.
   It was ⁵_____ to see you / everybody.

   Making future plans
   Let's do this / meet up ⁶_____ soon.
   ⁷_____ go out to a restaurant.
   ⁸_____ to our house for dinner.
   When are you free ⁹_____?
   ¹⁰_____ you next Saturday / next week.
   That _____ great!

4. Cover the Key Language box. Write the words in the correct order to make sentences.
   1. great / party! / a / What   **What a great party!**
   2. inviting / Thanks / me. / for _____
   3. to / was / you. / great / It / see _____
   4. are / When / next? / free / you _____
   5. great / That / sounds! _____
   6. for / Come / house / our / to / dinner. _____
   7. was / so / That / much / fun! _____
   8. you / week. / See / next _____

YOUR TURN

5. Work with a partner. Write the messages.
   1. Student A: you went to Student B's party. Write a message to your partner. Say something good about the party. Give or send the message to Student B.
   2. Student B: answer Student A's message. Suggest meeting again.
   3. Student A: say yes. Make a future plan.
   4. Student B: say yes to the plan.

6. Start a new message thread. This time Student B went to Student A's house for dinner. Student B writes the first message.

87

Video 6: What did you do?

6 What did you do?

1. Work with a partner. What activities do you usually do in your free time?

2. Tell your partner:
   - The last time you did these activities, who with, and where
   - When you plan to do these activities next, who with and where

3. Look at the activities in the pictures. Put them in order for the ones you like most and least.

4. Read the text. Which activities are the most popular in the UK?

5. Read the text again and answer the questions.
   1. Do we have more free time than our parents and grandparents?
   2. Who watches the most live TV?
   3. What are the most popular on demand TV services?
   4. What is the difference in CD album sales from ten years ago to now?
   5. How many people watch music videos on YouTube?
   6. How long do most people spend on their phones every day in the UK?
   7. What other activities do we often do while using our phone?
   8. What are some people trying to stop at restaurant tables?

FREE TIME activities

watching TV

spending time with family and friends

listening to music

eating out

browsing the internet

Many people feel very busy now, but we actually have more free time than our parents and grandparents. So, what do we like doing with all this free time?

In the UK, two free time activities are very popular. The top two activities are watching TV and spending time with family and friends. Many older people still watch live TV, but many younger people watch on-demand services. In the UK, the three most popular services are Netflix, BBC iPlayer and Prime Video.

Two other popular free time activities are listening to music and browsing the internet. Listening to music is the third most popular free time activity in the UK. It's very different today from twenty years ago. About ten years ago, people bought around 120 million CDs a year, both physical and digital. Now it is only just over 40 million. Now, everyone streams music from Spotify, Apple and Amazon. Millions of people also watch music videos on YouTube.

The fifth most popular activity – browsing the internet – is also very different now. Just ten years ago nearly everyone accessed the internet from a desktop computer. Just six years later, mobile phones became the main way people access the internet. A typical person in the UK spends nearly three and a half hours a day on their phone. We often spend our time on phone screens while we are doing something else. For example, two thirds of people use their phone while they are watching TV, and one third use it while they are travelling to work.

One activity in the top five isn't to do with technology – it's eating out. This is the fourth most popular activity in the UK. Some people are trying hard to keep this activity free from technology. A lot of people now ban mobile phones at the table. In a restaurant, a lot of people have a rule that the first person to use their phone, pays for dinner for everyone!

6 Work with a partner. How long do you use your mobile phone each day? Do you think it's a good idea to ban phones while you are eating? Why?

7 Watch the first part of the video. Complete the five people's answers to the first question.
1 I went to the ....
2 Yesterday I .... It was very busy.
3 I went to a .... match. We lost.
4 I played .... with a friend. I won.
5 I watched .... on my laptop.

8 Watch the second part of the video. Match each person to an activity.
1 Daniel   a studied for an exam
2 Pepa   b did a job interview
3 Reice   c visited family
4 Elise   d performed in a play
5 Hervé   e visited a friend

9 Watch the third part of the video. Write the correct name for each question.
1 Who is going to work?
2 Who is going to spend time with friends?
3 Who is going to go to another town?

10 Watch the final part of the video. Match each person to an activity and a place.
1 Daniel   Peru   to see family
2 Pepa   give up smoking   to work
3 Reice   Spain   to study
4 Elise   act in a film
5 Hervé   America

11 Work with a partner. Ask and answer the questions from the video.
1 What did you do yesterday?
2 What did you do last weekend?
3 What are you going to do next weekend?
4 What are you going to do next year?

Review

LESSON 11A Name 2 phrases with each of these verbs: *do, go, get, have*.

LESSON 11B Write 6 verbs that are irregular in the Past Simple.

LESSON 11B Write 2 sentences to describe experiences you had recently. Use *difficult, boring, and interesting*.

LESSON 11B How are these Past Simple verbs pronounced? *closed, cooked, invited, asked, cleaned and started*

LESSON 11C Write 2 adjectives in each column to describe experiences.
Positive adjectives
Negatives adjectives
Neutral adjectives

LESSON 11C Write a brief review of a restaurant you ate in recently.

LESSON 12A Write 3 plans you have for next year. Use *be going to*.

LESSON 12A Complete the phrases with *do, get, go* or *move*: *travelling, a job, to university, in with friends*.

LESSON 12B Write one sentence about you using each of these tenses: Present Simple, Present Continuous, Past Simple, *be going to*.

LESSON 12B Write the opposite adjectives for these adjectives: *excited, happy*.

LESSON 12C Write 2 phrases you can use to finish a conversation.

LESSON 12C Write 2 WhatsApp messages to arrange to see someone again.

89

Grammar Reference

Unit 1

1B *Be*: I, you, he, she, it

I / you – Form

	I	you
+	I'm / I am from Italy.	You're/ You are from Italy.
-	I'm not / I am not from Germany.	You aren't / You are not Chinese.
?	Where am I?	Where are you from?
	Am I right?	Are you Chinese?

Contractions

We often use contractions with *be*:

I am French. = I'm French.
You are right. = You're right.

Short answers

We do not use contractions in positive short answers, but we can use contractions in negative short answers.

Am I late? Yes, you are. NOT ~~Yes, you're.~~ / No, you aren't.
Are you Spanish? Yes, I am. NOT ~~Yes, I'm.~~ / No, I'm not.

He / she / it – Form

	he / she / it
+	He's / He is from Brazil. She's / She is from Spain. It's / It is from Canada.
-	He isn't / He is not from Germany. She isn't / She is not from Austria. It isn't / It is not American.
?	Is he from France? Is she from Poland?

Word order in questions

Notice the word order in questions.

+ She is from Russia. → Is she from Russia?
  He is from Greece. → Is he from Greece?

Short answers

Is she from Russia? Yes, she is. / No, she isn't.
Is he from Greece? Yes, he is. / No, he isn't.
Is it good? Yes, it is. / No, it isn't.

Negative contractions

He is not. = He isn't. OR He's not.
She is not. = She isn't. OR She's not.

Unit 2

2A *Be*: all forms

Form

	I	he / she / it	you / we / they
+	I'm / I am from Italy.	He's / He is from Italy.	You're/ You are from Italy.
-	I'm not / I am not from Germany.	She isn't / She is not French.	We aren't / We are not Chinese.
?	Where am I?	Where is it from?	Where are they from?
	Am I right?	Is he American?	Are you Chinese?

Short answers

Am I right? Yes, I am. / No, I'm not.
Is she from Russia? Yes, she is. / No, she isn't.
Are we late? Yes, we are. / No, we aren't.

Negative contractions

I am not = I'm not.
It is not. = It isn't. OR It's not.
They are not. = They aren't. OR They're not.

2B Questions

Form

Question word	Verb	Subject	Answer
Who	is	Nick?	He's a friend.
What	is	your phone number?	It's 07792 343 581.
Where	are	you from?	I'm from Sydney in Australia.
When	is	the lesson?	It's at four o'clock.
How	are	you?	I'm fine, thanks.
How old	is	he?	He's 24.

Contractions

You can contract *is* after question words.

What**'s** her name? = What **is** her name?
Where**'s** he from? = Where **is** he from?
How**'s** Nicky? = How **is** Nicky?

We don't contract *is* in a question when the last word is a pronoun.

How old **is** she? NOT ~~How old's she?~~
Who **is** it? NOT ~~Who's it?~~

Unit 3

3A Singular and plural nouns; a / an

Singular nouns

We use *a / an* + singular noun.
We use *a* + word beginning with a consonant.

a brush   **a** book   **a** watch

We use **an** + word beginning with a vowel.

an apple   **an** umbrella

Plural nouns

We use a number or *some* + plural nouns.

two apples   **some** apples
two books   **some** books

Spelling rules

We add **-s** to most plurals.
We add **-es** to words ending in *ch, sh, s, ss* and *x*.
We change **-y** to **-ies** for words ending in *y*.

+ **-s**: two key**s**, three pen**s**
+ **-es**: two watch**es**, some bus**es**
+ **-ies**: two count**ries**, three cit**ies**

3B *This, that, these* and *those*

We use *this* and *these* for things near us. We use *this* for singular nouns and *these* for plural nouns.

This is my book.
These are my keys.

We use *that* and *those* for things further away. We use *that* for singular nouns and *those* for plural nouns.

That T-shirt is nice.
How much are **those** hats?

Unit 4

4A Possessives

Possessive adjectives

Subject pronoun	Possessive adjective	
I	my	I'm Spanish. **My** name is Juan.
you	your	**You** are English. **Your** name is John.
he	his	**He** is 18. **His** birthday is tomorrow.
she	her	**She** is Italian. **Her** family is from Rome.
it	its	**It** is a Spanish restaurant. **Its** name is Quattro.
we	our	**We** are from Australia. **Our** names are Luke and Fiona.
they	their	**They** are from Russia. **Their** names are Vladimir and Olga.

Possessive 's

We add 's to a name or singular noun to say that something belongs to someone.

Is that Sam**'s** bag?
This is the teacher**'s** pen.

It's or Its?

It's = It is. **It's** a French restaurant.
Its = possessive. **Its** name is Le Chat Noir.

4B Adjectives; have / has

Adjectives

We use adjectives to describe things and people. Adjectives come <u>after</u> the verb. But they come <u>before</u> the noun.

My house **is small**. NOT ~~My house small is.~~
The potatoes **are old**.
It's a **beautiful day**. NOT ~~It's a day beautiful.~~
Joe has a **new car**.

Have / has

Have is a common irregular verb.

Form

	I / you / we / they	he / she / it
+	I **have** a new phone.	He **has** a new phone.
−	We **don't have** a new phone.	She **doesn't have** a new phone.
?	**Do you have** a new phone?	**Does he have** a new phone?

Use

We use *have/has* to talk about possession.

I **have** a car and a house.
My brother **doesn't have** a house, but he **has** an apartment.
Do you have a car and a house?

Unit 5

5A Present Simple positive and negative: *I, you, we, they*

Form

In positive sentences, the Present Simple form is the same for *I, you, we* and *they*.

Subject	Verb	
I		
You	**play**	tennis.
We		
They		

Negatives

We use *do + not* (*don't*) + verb to make negatives.

I / You / We / They **don't play** tennis.
I / You / We / They **don't go** cycling.

Use

We use the Present Simple to talk about things we usually do.

I **do** yoga on Saturdays.
We **play** tennis every Saturday.

5B Present Simple questions: *I, you, we, they*

Form

Questions	Short answers
Do you work?	Yes, I **do**. / No, I **don't**.
Do they have children?	Yes, they **do**. / No, they **don't**.
Do I need a car?	Yes, you **do**. / No, you **don't**.
Do we have a flat?	Yes, we **do**. / No, we **don't**.

Unit 6

6A Adverbs of frequency

always	100%	I **always** get up at 7 o'clock.
usually		We **usually** visit my parents at the weekend.
often		I **often** work at the weekend.
sometimes		They **sometimes** go for a walk.
hardly ever		They **hardly ever** visit their grandparents.
never	0%	He **never** eats fish.

Adverbs of frequency go before the main verb.

They **always have** a shower in the morning.
NOT ~~Always I have a shower in the morning.~~ OR ~~I have always a shower in the morning.~~

6B Present Simple: *he, she, it*

Form

For the Present Simple of regular verbs with *he, she* or *it*, we add -s to the verb.

We use *doesn't* with negatives and *does* with questions.

+	-	?	Short answers
He work**s**.	He **doesn't** work.	**Does** he work?	Yes, he **does**. / No, he **doesn't**.
She work**s**.	She **doesn't** work.	**Does** she work?	Yes, she **does**. / No, she **doesn't**.
It work**s**.	It **doesn't** work.	**Does** it work?	Yes, it **does**. / No, it **doesn't**.

Look at the word order in *Wh-* questions.

Where does he live?

Spelling

With most verbs, we add -s.

He work**s** in a school.
She play**s** tennis.

With verbs ending in -ch, -sh, -ss or -x, we add -es.

He watch**es** TV every evening.
She finish**es** work at 6 pm.
He go**es** to work at eight in the morning.
The weather chang**es** every year.
He fix**es** TVs.

With some verbs ending in -y, we add -ies.

She stud**ies** French.

Irregular verbs

Some verbs are irregular in the *he/she/it* form.

He **has** two brothers.
She **does** a lot of work.
He **goes** to work by bus.

Unit 7

7A *Like / love / hate* + verb + *-ing*

Form

We can use as *like, love, don't like, hate* + the *-ing* form of a verb.

I **love**	**playing** football.
I **like**	**eating** pizza.
I **don't like**	**watching** TV.
I **hate**	**working** in the evening.

Use

We use *love / like* + *-ing* for positive feelings.
We use *don't like / hate* for negative feelings.

Spelling rules

With most verbs, we add *-ing* to the infinitive.

  play > **playing**   listen > **listening**

With verbs ending in *-e*, we remove the *-e* and add *-ing*.

  take > **taking**   live > **living**

With some verbs that end in a vowel + a consonant, we double the consonant and add *-ing*.

  swim > **swimming**

With verbs ending in *l*, we double the *l*.

  travel > **travelling**

7B Word order in questions

Questions with *be*

The position of the verb *be* changes in questions.

+	?
He's French.	**Is he** French?
It is eight o'clock.	What time **is it**?
They are late.	**Are they** late?

Present Simple questions

+	?
They speak Spanish.	**Do they speak** Spanish?
He lives in Belgium.	Where **does he live**?

Unit 8

8A *some* and *any*

Positive sentences

In positive sentences we use *some* with uncountable nouns and with plural nouns. We use *a/an* with singular countable nouns.

We need **some** cheese and we need **some** oranges.
We also need **an** onion.

Negative sentences

In negative sentences we use *any* with uncountable nouns and with plural nouns. We use *a/an* with singular countable nouns.

We don't have **any** pasta and we don't have **any** tomatoes.
We don't have **an** egg.

Questions

In questions we use *any* with uncountable nouns and with plural nouns. We use *a/an* with singular nouns.

Do we have **any** rice?
Do we need **any** apples?
Do you have **a** red pepper?

8B *Can* and *can't*

Form

Can and *can't* are the same for all subjects.

+	I **can** cook. She **can** play the guitar.
-	He **can't** speak French. I **can't** ride a bike.
?	**Can you** come to my house? **Can she** play tennis?

Use

We use *can* and *can't* to talk about ability.

I **can** drive.
She **can't** speak Italian.

Unit 9

9A Present Continuous

Form

We form the Present Continuous with the correct form of *be* + verb + *-ing*.

	I	he / she / it	you / we / they
+	I'**m reading** a book.	He**'s reading** a book.	They**'re reading** a book.
-	I**'m not reading** a book.	She **isn't reading** a book.	We **aren't reading** a book.
?	**Am** I **reading** a book?	**Is** he **reading** a book?	**Are** they **reading** a book?

Spelling rules

With most verbs, we add *-ing* to the infinitive.

play > **playing**   listen > **listening**

With verbs ending in *-e*, we remove the *-e* and add *-ing*.

take > **taking**   live > **living**

With verbs ending in a vowel + a consonant, we double the consonant and add *-ing*.

swim > **swimming**   plan > **planning**

With verbs ending in *l*, we double the *l*.

travel > **travelling**

Use

We use the Present Continuous to talk about things that are happening now.

I**'m having** a shower.
They**'re playing** computer games.

9B Present Simple and Present Continuous

Present Simple – Use

We use the Present Simple to talk about things that are true, or things that usually happen.

I **live** in Norway.
I **travel** to London every month.
I **don't like** bananas.
We **don't play** tennis very often.

Present Continuous – Use

We use the Present Continuous to talk about things that are happening now.

I**'m staying** with my parents at the moment.
He **is visiting** his cousins now.
What **are** you **doing**?

Some verbs are state verbs. We do not usually use these in the Present Continuous. Examples of state verbs are *like, love, hate, want, have, own*.

I **like** hip hop music.   NOT I'm liking hip hop music.
I **want** to go on holiday.   NOT I'm wanting to go on holiday.
I **have** two sisters.   NOT I'm having two sisters.

Unit 10

10A There is / there are

Form

Positive

There	is	a café. (singular)
	are	some shops. (plural)

Negative

There	isn't	a garden.
	aren't	any shops.

Yes/no questions			Short answers
Is	there	a café?	Yes, **there is**. / No, **there isn't**.
Are		any shops?	Yes, **there are**. / No, **there aren't**.

Note that we often use *any* in questions with *Are there …?*

Are there any chairs?

We can contract *there is* (*there's*) but we don't contract *there are*.

There's a big desk next to the bed.
There's a plant on the coffee table.
There are three chairs.

10B Was / were

Form

	I / he / she / it	you / we / they
+	He **was** busy.	They **were** busy.
-	He **wasn't** busy.	They **weren't** busy.
?	**Was** it a good party?	**Were** you busy?
	Yes, it **was**. / No, it **wasn't**.	Yes, we **were**. / No, we **weren't**.

Use

We use *was / were* to talk about things in the past.

I **was** late.
He **wasn't** at home yesterday.
They **were** at work yesterday evening.
There **weren't** many restaurants.

Unit 11

11A Past Simple: Common irregular verbs

Form

Irregular verbs change their form in the positive form of the Past Simple.

We use *didn't* + verb in Past Simple negatives and *did* + verb in Past Simple questions.

Many very common verbs are irregular in English so it is important to learn their forms.

Please see the Irregular verb table on page 106 for a full list.

Verb	Positive	Negative	Question
go	I **went** to work.	I **didn't go** to work.	**Did** I **go** to work?
get	She **got** up late.	She **didn't get** up late.	**Did** she **get** up late?
have	They **had** a cat.	They **didn't have** a cat.	**Did** they **have** a cat?

Questions and answers

Did they have a party?
Yes, they **did**. / No they **didn't**.
Did he go to work?
Yes, he **did**. / No, he **didn't**.

Use

We use the Past Simple to talk about actions in the past.

I **went** to work yesterday.
They **had** a party last weekend.

11B Past Simple: Regular verbs

Form

The form of the Past Simple is the same for all subjects.
In Past Simple negatives, we use *didn't* + verb.
In Past Simple questions, we use *did* + verb.

Positive	Negative	Question
I **walked** to the shops.	I **didn't walk** to the shops.	**Did** I **walk** to the shops?
She **loved** the book.	She **didn't love** the book.	**Did** she **love** the book?
They **studied** French.	They **didn't study** French.	**Did** they **study** French?

Questions and answers

Did she walk to the shops?
Yes, she **did**. / No she **didn't**.
Did they study French?
Yes, they **did**. / No, they **didn't**.

Spelling rules

With most verbs we add *-ed*.

work > **worked**   start > **started**

With verbs ending in *-e,* we add *-d*.

love > **loved**   like > **liked**

With verbs ending in a consonant + *-y*, we remove the *-y* and add *ied*.

study > **studied**   marry > **married**

Use

We use the Past Simple to talk about actions in the past.

I **played** football last Sunday.
They **finished** their drinks and **walked** home.

Unit 12

12A *Be going to*

Form

	I	he / she / it	you / we / they
+	I'**m going to buy** a house	He'**s going to buy** a house.	They'**re going to buy** a house.
-	I'**m not going to play** tennis.	He **isn't going to play** tennis.	We **aren't going to play** tennis.
?	**Am** I **going to work** this weekend?	**Is** he **going to work** this weekend?	**Are** you **going to work** this weekend?

Use

We use *be going to* to talk about future plans and intentions.

Sam i**s going to play** football on Saturday.
We **aren't going to go** on holiday this year.
What **are** you **going to do** on Sunday?

Unit 12B Tense review

Tense	Example	Use
Present Simple	I **live** in Spain. She **doesn't do** any sports.	things that are true, or things that usually happen
Present Continuous	They **are working** at home today.	things that are happening now
Past Simple	We **saw** her last weekend. We **didn't see** her yesterday.	actions in the past
Be going to	We'**re going to watch** a film next weekend.	future plans and intentions

97

Communication Bank

1C Speaking, Exercise 6

Student A

1 Spell the names to your partner.
  1 Jenny Thompson
  2 Wei Yu
  3 Pedro Martinez

2 Write the names your partner spells.
  1 ....
  2 ....
  3 ....

2A Exercise 12

Student A

1 Where are the people from? Write the nationalities.

Where are they from?

Agnieszka Radwanska
She is ....

Penelope Cruz and Javier Bardem
They are ....

Shaun Mendes
He is ....

Neymar
He is ......Brazilian...... .

Andrew Lincoln
He is ....

Meghan Markle
She is ....

Chris and Luke Hemsworth
They are ....

2 Look at your answers to the quiz.
  Shaun Mendes is Canadian.
  Andrew Lincoln is British.
  Chris and Luke Hemsworth are Australian.

3 Ask your partner questions to find out the other answers.

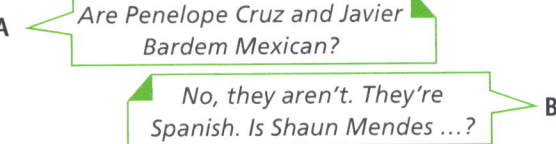

A: Are Penelope Cruz and Javier Bardem Mexican?

B: No, they aren't. They're Spanish. Is Shaun Mendes …?

4C Speaking, Exercise 6

Student A

1
- You are in the office.
- Ask about the time.

2
- You are at the bus stop.
- Ask about the time. Start with 'Excuse me'.
- Say you are late for a dinner date.
- Ask about the time of the next bus.

3
- You are in a restaurant.
- You are late. Say sorry.
- Say sorry again.

4
- You are in the office.
- Look at the time.
- Answer your partner's question.

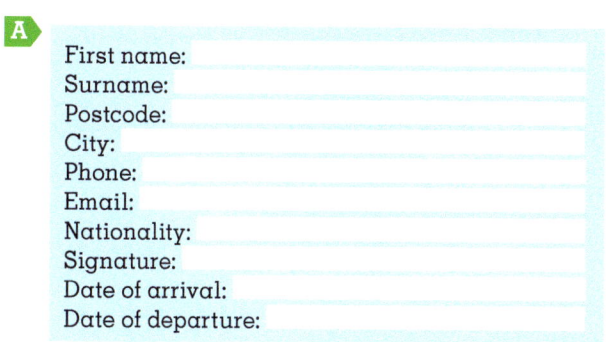

5
- You are at the train station.
- Look at the time.
- Answer your partner's question.
- The next train is at 8:10.

6
- You are in a restaurant.
- Look at the time.
- Your partner is twenty minutes late.

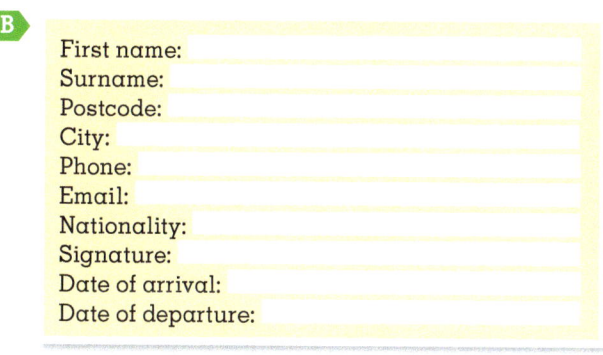

6C Speaking, Exercise 8

Student A

1 You are a hotel guest. Your name is Tony Costa.
- Ask to check in.
- Ask about breakfast (time).
- Ask about WiFi.

2 You are a hotel receptionist. A guest asks to check in. Use this information in your conversation.
- Ask the guest to fill in a form.
- The guest is in room 679 (sixth floor).
- Lift ✓ (over there).
- Swimming pool ✓ (opens 9 am).

6C Writing, Exercise 5

Student A

1 Complete hotel form A with information about you. Think of some dates for your hotel stay.

A
First name:
Surname:
Postcode:
City:
Phone:
Email:
Nationality:
Signature:
Date of arrival:
Date of departure:

2 Work with a partner. Take turns to ask and answer questions. Complete form B with information about your partner.

What's your first name?

B
First name:
Surname:
Postcode:
City:
Phone:
Email:
Nationality:
Signature:
Date of arrival:
Date of departure:

3 Compare forms with your partner. Did you write the information correctly?

7C Speaking, Exercise 7

Student A

1 Use the information to answer your partner's questions.

Ticket	A single to Venice
Price	18 euros
Time of the next train	11:35
Platform	8
Arrival time	12: 50

2 Ask questions to complete the table.

Ticket	A return to Lyon
Price	
Time of the next train	
Platform	
Arrival time	

8A Exercise 13

Student A

1 Complete the sentences for you.

THE FOOD I EAT

For breakfast I usually eat some .... and I drink some ....
For lunch I usually eat some ....
For dinner I often eat some .... or some ....
I don't eat any ....
I don't drink any ....

2 Work with a partner. Take turns to ask and answer questions. Which of your answers are similar?

> What do you eat for breakfast?

> I usually eat …

> Do you drink any cola?

8C Speaking, Exercise 6

Student A

1 You are a customer in a shop. Ask for:
   - potatoes (1 kilo)
   - tomatoes
   - a piece of Edam cheese (200 grams)
2 You work in a shop. Serve the customer.
   - You have salmon.
   - You don't have sushi.
   - You have rice – white and brown.

9C Speaking, Exercise 6

Student A

1 You are waiting for your work colleague, Student B, outside a meeting room.
   - Call your colleague.
   - Ask where he/she is.
2 You are in your car. You are meeting a friend, Student B, at a restaurant. There are lots of cars on the road. Student B calls you.
   - Say you are sorry.
   - Explain that you are driving down Henry Street.
   - Say you can be there in five minutes.

12C Speaking, Exercise 7

Student A

1 You are going to go to the cinema to meet your sister. You see a friend in the street.
   - Your friend says hello – you say hello.
   - Say how you are.
   - Say you can't go to the swimming pool and say why.
   - Say yes to his/her future plan.

2 You are with a colleague (Jack) in a café. You see another colleague there.
   - Say hello first.
   - Ask how your colleague is.
   - Introduce your colleague to Jack.
   - Say goodbye.

1C Speaking, Exercise 6

Student B

1 Write the names your partner spells.
   1 ....
   2 ....
   3 ....

2 Spell the names to your partner.
   1 Sally Hartman
   2 Dwayne Johnston
   3 Zoe Walker

2A Exercise 12

Student B

1 Where are the people from? Write the nationalities.

Where are they from?

Agnieszka Radwanska
She is ....

Penelope Cruz and Javier Bardem
They are ....

Shaun Mendes
He is ....

Neymar
He is ......Brazilian...... .

Andrew Lincoln
He is ....

Meghan Markle
She is ....

Chris and Luke Hemsworth
They are ....

2 Look at your answers to the quiz.
   Penelope Cruz and Javier Bardem are Spanish.
   Meghan Markle is American.
   Agnieszka Radwanska is Polish.

3 Ask your partner questions to find out the other answers.

A: Are Penelope Cruz and Javier Bardem Mexican?

B: No, they aren't. They're Spanish. Is Shaun Mendes …?

3B, Exercise 10

Student B

1 Look at the prices on your picture.
2 Ask Student A questions to find the missing prices.

   How much is this ...?
   How much is that ...?
   How much are these ...?
   How much are those ...?

3 Add the missing prices to your picture.

4
- You are in the office.
- Ask about the time.

5
- You are at the train station.
- Ask about the time. Start with 'Excuse me'.
- Say you are late for a dinner date.
- Find out the time of the next train.

6
- You are in a restaurant.
- You are late. Say sorry.
- Say sorry again..

4C Speaking, Exercise 7

Student B

1
- You are in the office.
- Look at the time.
- Answer your partner's question.

2
- You are at the bus stop.
- Look at the time.
- Answer your partner's question.
- The next bus is at 7:05.

3
- You are in a restaurant.
- Look at the time.
- Your partner is fifteen minutes late.

6C Speaking, Exercise 8

Student B

1 You are a hotel receptionist. A guest asks to check in. Use this information in your conversation.
- Ask the guest to fill in a form.
- The guest is in room 107 (first floor).
- Breakfast = 6.30 – 10.30.
- WiFi ✓ (login and password in guest's room)

2 You are a hotel guest. Your name is Jo Patterson.
- Ask to check in.
- Ask about a lift.
- Ask about the swimming pool (when open?).

6C Writing, Exercise 5

Student B

1 Complete hotel form A with information about you. Think of some dates for your hotel stay.

A
First name:
Surname:
Postcode:
City:
Phone:
Email:
Nationality:
Signature:
Date of arrival:
Date of departure:

2 Work with a partner. Take turns to ask and answer questions. Complete form B with information about your partner.

> What's your first name?

B
First name:
Surname:
Postcode:
City:
Phone:
Email:
Nationality:
Signature:
Date of arrival:
Date of departure:

3 Compare forms with your partner. Did you write the information correctly?

8A Exercise 13

Student B

1 Complete the sentences for you.

THE FOOD I EAT
For breakfast I usually eat some _____ and I drink some _____.
For lunch I usually eat some _____.
For dinner I often eat some _____ or some _____.
I don't eat any _____.
I don't drink any _____.

2 Work with a partner. Take turns to ask and answer questions. Which of your answers are similar?

> What do you eat for breakfast?
>> I usually eat …
>
> Do you drink any cola?

8C Exercise 6

Student B

1 You work in a shop. Serve the customer.
   - You have potatoes.
   - You don't have tomatoes.
   - You have Edam cheese.

2 You are a customer in a shop. Ask for:
   - salmon (four pieces)
   - sushi
   - some rice

9C Speaking, Exercise 6

Student B

1 You are going to a work meeting. It starts very soon. Your colleague, Student A, calls you.
   - Say you are finishing your coffee.
   - Say you can be there in one minute.
2 You are waiting for your friend, Student A. Call your friend.
   - Tell him/her that he/she is 25 minutes late.
   - Say you are waiting outside the restaurant.
   - Ask him/her to hurry up.

12C Speaking, Exercise 7

Student B

1 You are going to the swimming pool. You see a friend in the street.
   - Say hello first.
   - Ask how your friend is.
   - Say where you are going and ask if your friend wants to come.
   - Make a future plan.

2 You see a work colleague in a café. He/she is with a man you don't know.
   - Your colleague says hello – you say hello.
   - Say how you are.
   - Greet the new person, then look at your watch – say that you are late for a meeting.
   - Say goodbye.

Irregular verbs

The following irregular verbs are used very often in English. It's really important to learn them. Write in a translation of the infinitives to help you remember what each verb means.

Infinitive (without to)	Translation	Past Simple	Past Participle	Infinitive (without to)	Translation	Past Simple	Past Participle
be	....	was/were	been	leave	....	left	left
become	....	became	became	lose	....	lost	lost
begin	....	began	begun	make	....	made	made
break	....	broke	broken	meet	....	met	met
bring	....	brought	brought	pay	....	paid	paid
build	....	built	built	put	....	put	put
buy	....	bought	bought	read /riːd/	....	read /red/	read /red/
catch	....	caught	caught	ride	....	rode	ridden
choose	....	chose	chosen	run	....	ran	run
come	....	came	come	say	....	said	said
cost	....	cost	cost	see	....	saw	seen
cut	....	cut	cut	sell	....	sold	sold
do	....	did	done	send	....	sent	sent
drink	....	drank	drunk	shut	....	shut	shut
eat	....	ate	eaten	sing	....	sang	sung
fall	....	fell	fallen	sit	....	sat	sat
feel	....	felt	felt	sleep	....	slept	slept
fight	....	fought	fought	speak	....	spoke	spoken
find	....	found	found	spend	....	spent	spent
fly	....	flew	flown	stand	....	stood	stood
forget	....	forgot	forgotten	steal	....	stole	stolen
get	....	got	got	swim	....	swam	swum
give	....	gave	given	take	....	took	taken
go	....	went	gone/been	tell	....	told	told
grow	....	grew	grown	think	....	thought	thought
have	....	had	had	understand	....	understood	understood
hear	....	heard	heard	wake	....	woke	woken
hit	....	hit	hit	wear	....	wore	worn
keep	....	kept	kept	win	....	won	won
know	....	knew	known	write	....	wrote	written
learn	....	learnt/learned	learnt/learned				

Audio Scripts

Unit 1
Track 007

1
Michael: Hello, I'm Michael. What's your name?
Meiko: Hi, I'm Meiko.
Michael: Nice to meet you.
Meiko: Nice to meet you, too.
Michael: Where are you from, Meiko?
Meiko: I'm from Japan.
Michael: Oh, are you from Tokyo?
Meiko: No, I'm not. I'm from Osaka.

2
Diane: Hello, I'm Diane.
Tim: Hi, I'm Tim.
Diane: Nice to meet you.
Tim: Nice to meet you, too.
Diane: Where are you from?
Tim: I'm from the USA.
Diane: Oh, where in the USA?
Tim: From New York.

3
David: Hello, I'm David.
Ana: Hi, I'm Ana.
David: Nice to meet you.
Ana: Nice to meet you, too.
David: Are you from Brazil?
Ana: Yes, I am.
David: Oh, where in Brazil?
Ana: From São Paulo.

4
Lucy: Hello, I'm Lucy.
Fred: Hi, I'm Fred.
Lucy: Nice to meet you.
Fred: Nice to meet you, too.
Lucy: Where are you from?
Fred: I'm from Germany.
Lucy: Ah, I think you're from Berlin. Am I right?
Fred: Yes, you are.

Track 009

Michael: Hello, I'm Michael. What's your name?
Meiko: Hi, I'm Meiko.
Michael: Nice to meet you.
Meiko: Nice to meet you, too.
Michael: Where are you from, Meiko?
Meiko: I'm from Japan.
Michael: Oh, are you from Tokyo?
Meiko: No, I'm not. I'm from Osaka.

Track 010

Luca: Hi, I'm Luca.
Maria: Hi, I'm Maria.
Luca: Are you from Spain?
Maria: No, I'm not. I'm from Portugal.
Luca: Where in Portugal?
Amelie: I'm from Porto. Where are you from?
Luca: I'm from England.
Amelie: Are you from London?
Luca: Yes, I am.

Track 011

1
A: This is Justin Bieber.
B: Where is he from?
A: He's from Canada.

2
A: This is Rihanna.
B: Is she from America?
A: No, she isn't. She's from Saint Michael. It's in Barbados.

Track 014

1 /ei/ a, h, j, k
2 /ee/ b, c, d, e, g, p, t, v
3 /e/ f, l, m, n, s, x, z
4 /ai/ i, y
5 /oh/ o
6 /u/ q, u, w
7 /ah/ r

Track 015

1
A: Hello.
B: Good afternoon.
A: My name is Rob Francis. I have a table for two at eight o'clock.
B: What's your first name?
A: Rob: r-o-b.
B: And what's your surname?
A: Francis.
B: How do you spell that?
A: f-r-a-n-c-i-s
B: Thank you. Come this way. Here's your table.
2
A: Hello.
B: Good afternoon.
A: My name is John Jameson. I have a reservation.
B: Sorry, what's your first name?
A: John.
B: How do you spell that?
A: J-o-h-n.
B: And what's your surname?
A: Jameson: j-a-m-e-s-o-n
B: Thank you. Yes, you're in room 301.

Track 017

A seven
B three
C fifteen
D twenty
E two
F twelve
G nine
H nineteen
I six
J sixteen

Track 018

1 one, two …
2 thirteen, fourteen …
3 five, six …
4 seventeen, eighteen …
5 three, four …
6 ten, eleven …
7 nine, ten …
8 fifteen, sixteen …

Track 019

1
A: What's your phone number?
B: 07996542831
2
A: What's your phone number?
B: 01286 505 734
3
A: What's your phone number?
B: 0044 1249863745

Track 020

1
A: What's your name?
B: It's Ben Patterson.
A: How do you spell that?
B: p-a-t-t-e-r-s-o-n
2
A: What's your phone number?
B: It's 07992 543 675
A: Can you say that again, please?
B: Sure. It's 07992 543 675.

Unit 2
Track 030

1 His name is Sam. He's from Scotland. He's Scottish.
2 Her name is Ana. She's from Spain. She's Spanish.
3 It's from Italy. It's Italian.
4 They're from China. They're Chinese.

Track 032

1 Mo Salah is Egyptian.
2 Reese Witherspoon is American.
3 Salma Hayek is Mexican.
4 Marion Cotillard is French.
5 Jürgen Klopp is German.
6 Jose Mourinho is Portuguese.

Track 035

Jack:	Hello. I'm Jack Mullins.
Ana:	Nice to meet you, Jack. I'm Ana and this is Alex.
Jack:	Nice to meet you, too. Are you American?
Alex:	No, we aren't. We are Mexican. Are you American?
Jack:	No, I'm not American – I am from Oxford. I'm British. But my mum and dad are from Nice.
Ana:	Nice is in France – am I right?
Jack:	Yes, you are.
Alex:	So, they are French.
Jack:	Yes, they are.

Track 036

1	businessman
2	police officer
3	firefighter
4	teacher
5	chef
6	doctor
7	waiter
8	businesswoman
9	nurse

Track 037

A:	What's your name?
B:	My name's Chang.
A:	What's your job?
B:	I'm a businessman.
A:	How old are you?
B:	I'm 29. What's your name?

Track 039

1	18
2	60
3	31
4	17
5	27
6	99

Track 040

Edward:	My name is Edward Smith and I'm 35.
Rosie:	Hi, Edward.
Edward:	Hello! What's your name?
Rosie:	I'm Rosie Baker.
Edward:	Hi, Rosie. How old are you?
Rosie:	I'm 28 and I'm a teacher. What's your job?
Edward:	I'm a doctor.
Rosie:	A doctor! Wow! What's your phone number?
Edward:	It's 07279 72283954.

Track 041

Rosie:	Hello. Edward?
Edward:	Er … Yes. Who is it?
Rosie:	It's Rosie.
Edward:	Oh, hi, Rosie. How are you?
Rosie:	I'm fine, thanks. Er … so … my birthday party is this weekend. Are you free?
Edward:	Erm … when is the party?
Rosie:	It's on Saturday, at 8 pm.
Edward:	OK … and where is it?
Rosie:	It's in London, at Bar Pepito, at King's Cross.
Edward:	Oh … er, so the name of the bar … how do you spell it?
Rosie:	So, it's Bar Pepito – P – E – P – I – T – O. Are you free?
Edward:	Erm … yes, I am.
Mum:	Who's that on the phone, Ed?
Rosie:	Who is that? Are you married?
Edward:	No, I'm not. It's my mum.
Rosie:	Oh … OK. Look – what's your email address? I can email the information to you.
Edward:	OK – it's e_smith@tmail.com.
Rosie:	Thanks, Ed … see you on Saturday. Bye.
Edward:	Bye.

Track 042

1
Edward: Who is it?
Rosie: It's Rosie.
2
Edward: How are you?
Rosie: I'm fine, thanks.
3
Edward: When is the party?
Rosie: It's on Saturday at 8 pm.
4
Edward: Where is it?
Rosie: It's in London.
5
Edward: How do you spell it?
Rosie: P-E-P-I-T-O
6
Rosie: What's your email address?
Edward: It's e_smith@tmail.com

Track 043

1. What's your name?
2. How do you spell that?
3. What's your address?
4. How old are you?
5. Who's your best friend?
6. What's your job?
7. When's your birthday?
8. What's your email address?

Track 044

1
A: Good morning.
B: Good morning. Two white coffees, please.
A: Of course.
2
A: Goodbye! See you next week.
B: Bye, Kate.
3
A: Excuse me. Can I get past?
B: Oh. I'm sorry.
4
A: Here's your card. Have a nice day.
B: Thanks. And you.
5
A: Goodnight. Sleep well.
B: Goodnight, mum.

Track 045

1
A: Good evening.
B: Good evening. A table for two, please.
2
A: Good morning, Jake! How are you?
B: Fine, thanks. And you?
3
A: Bye, Jane.
B: Bye, Luke. See you tomorrow.
4
A: Excuse me!
B: I'm sorry.
5
A: Goodnight.
B: Goodnight. Sleep well.
6
A: Here's your card. Have a nice day.
B: Thanks. And you.

Unit 3
Track 049

1. four brushes
2. two watches
3. a bag
4. a laptop
5. a notebook
6. some pencils
7. a bank card
8. some desks
9. some keys
10. an umbrella
11. a pen
12. a wallet
13. two purses

Track 050

/s/ desks
/z/ pencils
/iz/ watches

Track 051

/s/ desks, wallets
/z/ pencils, keys
/iz/ watches, purses

Track 052

1. three phones
2. an email
3. two cities
4. some houses
5. two buses
6. a pizza
7. some tickets
8. a taxi

Track 054

1
Eva: What's in your pocket, Sam?
Sam: In my pocket I have my wallet and some keys.
2
Sam: What's in your bag, Eva?
Eva: In my bag I have a pen and my purse. And I have an umbrella.

Track 055

1. a coat
2. a dress
3. a T-shirt
4. a hat
5. some shoes
6. a jacket
7. some trousers
8. some jeans
9. a skirt
10. a shirt

Track 056

1. Ooh, look! That green dress is nice! How much is it?
2. I like those red shoes. But they're £200!
3. I like this blue hat. It's very nice! It's only £2!
4. Those trousers are lovely! How much are they?
5. Can I have one of those T-shirts? The grey one.
6. How much are these jeans?

Track 057

1. This red T-shirt isn't very nice!
2. Are those your clothes!
3. Is that your phone over there?
4. These are my children.
5. How much are those black hats?
6. How much is this blue shirt?

Track 058

1. twenty pence
2. fifty cents
3. ten euros
4. twenty dollars
5. twenty five cents
6. ten pounds

Track 059

1. four dollars ninety-nine cents
2. Seventy-five pence
3. fifty cents
4. five pounds eighty-five
5. twelve euros and ninety-eight cents
6. three euros and forty-five cents
7. two dollars eighty cents
8. one pound and thirty pence

Track 060

1
A: Can I have a black coffee, please?
B: There you go.
A: How much is it?
B: £1.85
2
A: Can I have a cheese sandwich, please?
B: There you go.
A: How much is it?
B: $4.50
3
A: Can I have a salad, please?
B: There you go.
A: How much is it?
B: €9.49

Track 061

Barista: Who's next?
Tim: Can I have a chicken wrap, please?
Barista: Anything else?
Tim: A black coffee, please.
Barista: There you go.
Tim: How much is it?
Barista: £5.75. Here's the machine.
Barista: Yes, that's fine. Thank you.

Track 062

A: Who's next?
B: Can I have a cheese sandwich, please?
A: Anything else?
B: And a cola, please.
A: There you go.
B: How much is it?
A: £7.85. Here's the machine.
A: Yes, that's fine. Thank you.

Unit 4
Track 065

1. Tom is a man.
2. Ben is a boy.
3. Ivy is a girl.
4. Eva is a woman.

Track 067

1. wife
2. mother
3. mum
4. husband
5. father
6. dad
7. parents
8. son
9. brother
10. daughter
11. sister

Track 070

Interviewer: So, tell us about your family, Prisha.
Prisha: Well, my husband Vikram is very clever. He's a teacher.
Dev: You're clever too Mum. You're a doctor!
Prisha: Thanks, Dev.
Dev: But you and Dad are old.
Prisha: Er, no. I'm 33 and Dad's 35 – we're not old! You're eight – so you're young!
Dev: No, I'm not. Mina is five – she's young, and she's funny.
Prisha: Yes, she is. And you're very clever, Dev.
Dev: Thanks, mum. I love school! But Dad says I'm lazy.
Prisha: Well, yes, you are lazy.
Dev: No, I'm not! I play football every day.
Prisha: But what about your school work?
Dev: Well, I'm clever, so it's fine.
Prisha: Mmm …

Track 072

1	cheap
2	expensive
3	new
4	old
5	ugly
6	beautiful
7	big
8	small

Track 073

1	My parents are old.
2	It's a beautiful dress.
3	The pens are cheap.
4	Roger has a young wife.
5	Her bag is small.
6	They are expensive watches.
7	My doctor's house is big.
8	My phone is new.

Track 074

Kelly: So … what's new? Well, I have a new apartment in Oxford, and I have two bedrooms – so, one is my office. I'm a writer and I have all my books in there. It's great. I don't have a garden, but there's a balcony, so I'm happy.

And what about Jack? Does he have some news? Well, yes he does … Jack has a girlfriend! Her name's Laura and she's a businesswoman. She has a job in London. She's beautiful and she's really funny!

And what about Rosie? Well, Rosie has a job, so she has money! So now she has an expensive hand bag, a Rolex watch and a new car! She doesn't have a boyfriend, but she is fine about that!

Oh, and our parents have a new house by the sea. It's for holidays. It's small but it's beautiful. And they have a new dog. Her name's Lucky and she's big and brown – and she's very clever.

Track 075

1	My parents have an old car.
2	Does your sister have a boyfriend?
3	We have an expensive car.
4	Her brother has an ugly dog.
5	Do you have a house by the sea?
6	I have a clever son.
7	Do you have a beautiful house?
8	I don't have a watch.

Track 077

Conversation 1
Luke: What time is it, Jane?
Jane: It's seven o'clock.
Luke: OK. Thanks. It's time to go home!

Conversation 2
Luke: Er. Excuse me. What's the time?
Man: It's half past seven.
Luke: Oh no! I'm late for my dinner date. What time is the next bus to the city centre?
Man: The next bus is at ten to eight.

Conversation 3
Luke: Oh, hi, Anna. Sorry I'm late!
Anna: Hi Luke. Yes, you're twenty-five minutes late!
Luke: I'm so sorry, Anna.
Anna: That's OK. Let's order some drinks.

Unit 5
Track 080

1	beach
2	shopping
3	basketball
4	board games
5	exercise
6	drama
7	computer games
8	tennis
9	cycling
10	cinema
11	running
12	swimming

Track 081

1	My friends and I like the beach. We go to the beach on Saturdays. It's fun!
2	I play tennis with my brother.
3	My parents are 65 and 67 years old, but they do exercise every day.
4	I play computer games online with my friends.
5	My sister and her boyfriend do a lot of sport. They go running three times a week.
6	Every Monday evening, I go swimming with my sister.

Track 082

Play board games, play computer games, play basketball, play tennis

Go swimming, go shopping, go running, go to the cinema, go to the beach, go cycling

Do exercise, do drama

Track 083

Nori I like sport. I do a lot of exercise. I play basketball and tennis and I go running once a week. My friends go cycling a lot. They go three times a week. I go cycling every Sunday afternoon with them.

Amy I like films. I go to the cinema a lot with my friends. In the summer, I also go to the beach a lot, but I don't go swimming in the sea. I don't like swimming! I don't do a lot of exercise but I do yoga once a week.

Track 085

A **A:** Do you have a brother or sister?
  B: Yes, I do. I have one brother.
B **A:** Do you want a coffee?
  B: No, thanks. I don't drink coffee.
C **A:** Do you speak German?
  B: No, I don't I only speak English.
D **A:** Do you have an umbrella? It's raining.
  B: Yes, I do. Here you go.

Track 086

1	live in a flat	6	read a book
2	drink coffee	7	listen to music
3	watch TV	8	eat breakfast
4	want a new car	9	speak English
5	have a cat		

Track 087

1 **A:** Where do you live?
  B: I live in Clapham, in South London. Where do you live?
  A: I live not far from you. I live in Balham. I have a flat there.
2 **A:** I work for one of the main banks. Who do you work for?
  B: I work for my parent's company.
  A: What do you do?
  B: I'm an accountant.
3 **A:** I play football for a local team. Do you play for a team?
  B: No, I don't, but I play five-a-side football with some friends every week.
  A: When do you play? At the weekend?
  B: No. I play every Monday at eight o'clock.
  A: Which team is your favourite?
  B: Manchester United.
  A: Me, too!
4 **A:** Do you have any brothers and sisters?
  B: I have two sisters.
  A: Who do you spend time with at the weekend?
  B: My sister, Anya. She's 19 and I'm 18.

Unit 6
Track 090

1	never
2	sometimes
3	often
4	usually
5	always

Track 092

/s/ gets, drinks
/z/ has, cycles, does
/ɪz/ washes

Track 093

/s/ gets, drinks, takes, likes, eats, checks
/z/ has, cycles, does, goes, leaves, buys
/ɪz/ washes, watches

Track 094

1
A: What does Jennifer Aniston do for 40 minutes?
B: She does yoga.
2
A: Where does Simon Cowell eat breakfast?
B: He eats breakfast in bed.
3
A: What time does Jennifer Aniston get up?
B: She gets up at 4.30 am.
4
A: Does Peter Jones buy a smoothie?
B: No, he doesn't buy a smoothie. He buys a coffee.
5
A: Does Peter Jones have a bath in the mornings?
B: No, he doesn't have a bath. He has a shower.
6
A: Does Kate Hudson take her children to school?
B: Yes, she does.
7
A: Does Simon Cowell eat eggs for breakfast?
B: No, he doesn't.
8
A: Does Kate Hudson watch TV in the mornings?
B: Yes, she does.

Track 095

1. breakfast
2. gym
3. swimming pool
4. lift
5. WiFi

Track 096

Julie: Good morning. Can I check into my room, please?
Receptionist: Of course. What's your name?
Julie: It's Julie White.
Receptionist: OK. Can you fill in this form, please?
Julie: Yes, of course.
Receptionist: Thank you. So, you're in room 302 on the third floor, Ms White. Here's your key card. The lift is over there.
Julie: Thanks. Is there WiFi in my room?
Receptionist: Yes, there is. The login and password are in your room.
Julie: Great. And what time is breakfast?
Receptionist: Breakfast is served from seven until ten in the dining room.
Julie: Thanks. And does the hotel have a gym?
Receptionist: Yes, it does, and a swimming pool.
Julie: What time does the gym open?
Receptionist: It opens at six o'clock in the morning.
Julie: Great. Thanks for your help.
Receptionist: You're welcome. Enjoy your stay.

Track 097

What the guest says
Can I check in to my room, please?
Is there WiFi in my room?
What time is breakfast?
Does the hotel have a gym?
What time does the gym open?

What the receptionist says
Can you fill in this form, please?
You're in room 302 on the third floor.
Here's your key card.
Breakfast is served from seven until ten.
It opens at 6 o'clock in the morning.
You're welcome. Enjoy your stay.

Unit 7
Track 099

1. I like eating out.
2. He likes playing the piano.
3. I like staying at home with my children.
4. We love going out in the evening.
5. We love walking in the countryside.
6. My boyfriend loves travelling.
7. I like relaxing in the park.
8. I love meeting my friends.

Track 100

Mia: My best friend is Sam. We both love cooking and eating out. We really love Italian food but we both hate flying. We often go on holiday together. We always go to a place with a good Italian restaurant!

Tom: My best friends are Ana and Harry. We don't like spending time at home and we like going out and doing things together. Both Harry and I like cycling and we often go on cycling holidays together.

Lisa: My best friend is my boyfriend, Tim. We both really like doing exercise. We often go to the gym together.

Track 101

1. Do you have a sister or brother?
2. Do you like Chinese food?
3. What music do you like?
4. When do you go to the gym?

Track 102

1. passenger
2. ticket office
3. ticket
4. platform
5. ticket machine

Track 103

A: A ticket to Paris, please.
B: Single or return?
A: A return, please.
B: For today?
A: Yes.
B: When do you want to come back?
A: Tomorrow morning. How much is it?
B: That's 49 euros.
A: What time is the next train?
B: It's at 14:50. The train leaves from platform 5.
A: What time does it arrive in Paris?
B: At sixteen thirty. Here's your ticket.
A: Great. Thank you.

Unit 8
Track 105

1. apples
2. cheese
3. salmon
4. sausages
5. bread
6. lettuce
7. bananas
8. eggs
9. strawberries
10. broccoli
11. beef
12. potatoes
13. chicken
14. tomatoes
15. cucumber
16. onions
17. pasta
18. rice
19. ham
20. avocado

Track 107

Louisa:	So, Ken. Do you like vegetables?
Ken:	No, I don't. But I like fruit.
Louisa:	Oh, OK. What fruit do you like?
Ken:	I like apples and strawberries. What about you, Louisa? Do you like vegetables?
Louisa:	Yes, I do. I love salad – so I like cucumber, lettuce and avocado.
Ken:	Salad! That's very healthy.
Louisa:	Yes, but I also eat a lot of meat. I love beef and chicken.
Ken:	Urgh – I don't like meat.
Louisa:	What about fish?
Ken:	No, I don't like fish. I'm a vegetarian.
Louisa:	You're a vegetarian, but you don't like vegetables!
Ken:	Yes! It's not great, is it!
Louisa:	But do you like cheese?
Ken:	Yes, I love cheese, and eggs. Oh, and I love pasta – I eat a lot of pasta!
Louisa:	I don't like pasta. I eat rice or potatoes with my meals.
Ken:	Mmm – I don't think dinner at your house is a good idea. We don't like the same foods!
Louisa:	No, we don't! Let's go to a restaurant.
Ken:	Good idea.

Track 108

What do famous people eat?

Every day, Prince Charles has a four-minute egg and some tea with milk for breakfast. He doesn't eat any food for lunch!

Meghan Markle has avocado on toast, with some olive oil for breakfast.

Boris Johnson loves sausages and eats them with some potatoes. And he drinks a litre of diet cola every day!

Mo Farah often has a chicken sandwich for lunch, then some fruit in the afternoon and usually salmon with some vegetables for dinner.

Does Victoria Beckham eat any cheese? No, but she eats some fish (usually sushi) every day.

Track 109

1	A:	What would you like to drink?
	B:	I'd like some water please.
2	A:	Do you have any cheese?
	B:	Yes. We have some cheddar.
3:	A:	Which sandwich would you like? Ham or chicken?
	B:	I don't eat any meat. Do you have any cheese sandwiches?
4	A:	Do you have any coffee?
	B:	No, we don't. But we have some tea.
5	A:	I don't have any lettuce for the salad, but I have some tomatoes and some cucumber.
	B:	Do you have any avocados?

Track 110

1 He can ride a bike.
2 She can swim.
3 He can dance.
4 He can lift 100 kilos.
5 She can sing.
6 He can play the piano.
7 She can speak Russian.
8 She can drive a bus.

Track 112

1
A: Can Lisa paint?
B: Yes, she can. She can paint really well.
2
A: Can she speak Spanish?
B: Yes, she can. She can speak Spanish fluently.
3
A: Can she cook?
B: No, she can't. She can't cook at all.
4
A: Can she drive?
B: No, she can't.
5
A: Can she ride a bike?
B: Yes, she can. She can ride a bike quite well.
6
A: Can she sing?
B: No, she can't. She can't sing at all.
7
A: Can she play the guitar?
B: Yes, she can. She can play the guitar really well.

Track 114

1
A: How can I help you?
B: Can I have some cheddar cheese, please?
A: Of course. How much would you like?
B: Just a small piece, please.
A: Is 100 grams OK?
B: Yes, that's fine.

2
A: Hello. Can I have 500 grams of onions, please?
B: Of course. Here you are. Anything else?
A: Yes. Do you have any avocados?
B: Yes, we do. How many would you like?
A: Two, please.

3
A: How can I help you?
B: I'd like three pieces of salmon, please.
A: Yes, sure. Anything else?
B: Do you have any ham?
A: No, we don't. Sorry.

Unit 9
Track 116

A	take a selfie
B	message friends
C	cook dinner
D	work on a laptop
E	clean my bedroom
F	do homework

Track 117

Nicola: Hi Jamie.
Jamie: Oh, hi, Nicola. How are you? What are you doing?
Nicola: Oh, I'm good. I'm sitting in my hotel room, working on my laptop. What are you doing? Are you cooking dinner?
Jamie: Yes, I am. I'm in the kitchen and I'm cooking pasta.
Nicola: And what's Sam doing? Is he watching TV?
Jamie: Er … no, he isn't watching TV.
Nicola: Is he playing computer games?
Jamie: No, he isn't! He's doing homework in the dining room.
Nicola: Oh, that's good. And what about Becky? What's she doing?
Jamie: She's in her bedroom. Becky – what are you doing? Your mum wants to know.
Becky: I'm messaging friends, Dad. Oh, and I'm cleaning my bedroom.
Jamie: She's messaging friends and she's cleaning her bedroom.
Nicola: Oh, good. Her bedroom is awful! Listen, can I call you again later? My dinner with my team is in five minutes.
Jamie: Of course. Have fun.

Track 118

1
A: Hi, Daniel. Are you doing your maths homework?
B: No, I'm not doing my homework. I'm cooking dinner for my parents.

2
A: You can't watch a film on TV because your dad is watching a football match.
B: He isn't watching a football match, Mum – he's cleaning the kitchen.

3
A: Look, that's my brother. He's talking on the phone.
B: Oh, yeah. And that's Ed next to him. He's drinking coffee.

4
A: Are your parents watching TV?
B: No, they aren't. They're working.

Track 121

1
Lucy: Jake – you're late! I'm waiting outside the office. The meeting starts in ten minutes!
Jake: I'm so sorry, Lucy. I'm finishing an email. I can be with you in one minute.
Lucy: OK. See you in a minute.

2
Su: Hi, Mike. Where are you? I'm sitting in the café, drinking juice. You're 20 minutes late!
Mike: I'm so sorry, Su. I'm driving down London Road and it's very busy! Can you wait ten minutes?
Su: OK. Hurry up!

3
Ed: Where are you? We're standing inside the festival area!
Rosie: I'm waiting outside the entrance. I'm waving!
Ed: Oh, yes. I can see you now!

Unit 10
Track 123

1. kitchen
2. garden
3. bathroom
4. dining room
5. living room
6. bedroom
7. toilet
8. garage
9. hall

Track 124

Caroline: These are the three places I like. A historic flat, a modern apartment and one house.
Ian: Let me see.
Caroline: This modern apartment is cheap.
Ian: It looks nice. There's space for six guests.
Caroline: There are three bedrooms. And there's a bathroom, a kitchen and a living room.
Ian: I like it. What other ones are there?
Caroline: This is the house.
Ian: Wow! That's big! It's also expensive!
Caroline: I know, but there's a really big garden! The kids love playing outside.
Ian: True. But there are four bedrooms. We only need three. Also, there's a toilet and there are three bathrooms! We don't need four toilets!
Caroline: I know, but it is beautiful. There's also a garage for the car.
Ian: True. Let me see the last one. That's a beautiful old building. So, it's a historic flat in an old building. How much is it?
Caroline: It's 1250 euros. There are three bedrooms, two bathrooms and a toilet. There isn't a dining room, but there is a table in the kitchen.
Ian: What about parking?
Caroline: There's on street parking.
Ian: OK. Let me see the modern apartment again. There's only one bathroom and there isn't another toilet. That's not enough for five of us. We have three children! Let's look at the big house and historic flat again.

Track 125

Caroline: Here's the big house again.
Ian: Can you show me the map? It's really far from the centre. There aren't any shops or restaurants near there.
Caroline: We can drive to the town.
Ian: Maybe. Show me the historic flat again.
Caroline: Here it is.
Ian: Can you show me the map? That looks better. Look, there are shops, restaurants, and cafés nearby.
Caroline: I know. It is really good for things to do but I love the garden.
Ian: I don't want to drive every day!
Caroline: You're right. OK, let's book this one.

Track 126

1. There are three bedrooms. A and C
2. There's also a garage for the car. B
3. There isn't a dining room but there is a table in the kitchen. C
4. There aren't any shops or restaurants near there. B

Track 127

1. We're at the cinema.
2. She's in hospital.
3. They're in a hotel by the sea.
4. We're in a restaurant.
5. They're in a museum.
6. They're at school.
7. I'm at the station.
8. They're in the swimming pool.
9. I'm in the supermarket.

Track 128

1
A: Where were you last night?
B: I was in London.
A: Were you with friends?
B: Yes, I was. We were in a cinema together.

2
A: Where were you last night?
B: I was on a train. My girlfriend was at the station waiting for me.
A: Were you home late?
B: Yes, we were. We work very late and my train was late! We get home about 10 o'clock most days.

3
A: Where were you last night?
B: I was out with my husband. It was his birthday and we were in the new Greek restaurant in town.
A: Was the restaurant good?
B: Yes, it was. It was excellent!

4
A: Where were you last night?
B: I was at home with my family.
A: Was there anything good on TV?
B: No, there wasn't. I think I was asleep by 11.

5
A: Where were you last night?
B: I was in the supermarket. I like doing my shopping late at night. It's usually very quiet. Last night there weren't many people there.

Track 129

1
A: Is there a café near here?
B: Yes, there's a café on North Road between the Chinese restaurant and the Irish bar.

2
A: Excuse me, where's the hospital?
B: It's at the end of West Road, on the right.

3
A: Is there a restaurant near here?
B: Yes, there's a restaurant on the corner of East Road and North street.

4
A: Is there a car park near here?
B: Yes, there's a car park on South Street, opposite the swimming pool.

5
A: Is there a park near here?
B: Yes. There's a park at the end of East Road, on the left.

6
A: Is there a bus station near here?
B: Yes, the bus station is on South Street, next to the train station.

Track 130

1. go straight on
2. turn left
3. turn right

Track 131

A: Excuse me. Is there a cash machine near here?
B: Yes, there's one on West Road.
A: Sorry, where is that?
B Go straight on and turn left on South Street. Go straight on until you see a supermarket and turn right onto West Road. There's a cash machine on your right. It's opposite the supermarket.
A: Thanks very much.
B: You're welcome.

Unit 11
Track 133

Sarah: What did you do on Sunday, Mark?

Mark: I had quite a lazy day! I got up at ten o'clock. I had a shower and then I phoned Amelia, my girlfriend. We had a coffee in a café at about 11 o'clock.

Sarah: That sounds nice! What did you do in the afternoon?

Mark: We went shopping in the city centre together.

Sarah: Did you buy any new clothes?

Mark: Yes, I did. I bought two new shirts for work! Amelia was busy in the evening so I went home at about five o'clock.

Sarah: Did you do anything interesting in the evening?

Mark: No, I didn't. I usually do sport on Sunday evenings, but I didn't do any sport yesterday. I was very tired. I had dinner, and then I did the housework.

Sarah: That's not fun!

Mark: I know. What about you? How was your Sunday? I saw all your photos on Instagram!

Sarah: Yes, I had a good time on Sunday. I posted a lot of photos!

Track 134

1
A: What time did you wake up this morning?
B: I woke up at 7:30.

2
A: When did you last catch a train?
B: I caught a train at the weekend.

3
A: How many coffees did you drink this morning?
B: I drank four coffees this morning.

4
A: Did you see your friends on Saturday?
B: Yes, I did. I saw Paul at a football match.

5
A: When did you last buy a present for someone?
B: I bought a new dress for my sister, for her birthday.

6
A: Did your parents come to your flat this weekend?
B: Yes, they did. They came for dinner on Saturday night.

7
A: What did you eat for breakfast this morning?
B: I ate some toast and cereal.

8
A: When did you leave home this morning?
B: I left at 8:30.

9
A: How long did you sleep last night?
B: I slept for eight hours.

Track 135

Rochelle: Hi Florence! How was China? Did you enjoy it?

Florence: Yes, I did. It was amazing! I loved it!

Rochelle: Where did you stay?

Florence: I stayed in Suzhou.

Rochelle: What did you do every day?

Florence: I studied Mandarin all morning. In the afternoon we learned about Chinese culture and history. I worked really hard, and the Mandarin lessons were very difficult. The afternoon was more fun. We didn't always work or study. Sometimes we just played Mahjong or watched Chinese TV!

Rochelle: That sounds fun! Did you have a lot of free time?

Florence: Yes, we did. At the weekends we didn't have any classes. So, we visited other cities in China.

Rochelle: What was your favourite city?

Florence: I loved Shanghai and Beijing. There was so much to see and do.

Rochelle: How long did you stay there?

Florence: I stayed there for three months. It was a really interesting and fun experience. How was your year in Liverpool Rochelle?

Rochelle: Well, the city is great. There are lots of old buildings next to the water. Ships came there in the past.

Florence: Cool.

Rochelle: Yeah, but you know they speak English there, and we speak English here in America?

Florence: Yes.

Rochelle: Well, I didn't understand people at first! I asked a woman for directions and when she answered, I didn't understand a word!

Florence: Really?!

Rochelle: Yes, the accent is so different. It was easier when I talked to other international students. After a few weeks though I understood people better.

Florence: Did you enjoy it there?

Rochelle: Yes, I did. I loved it! I made a lot of friends. It was difficult not living at home, though. I don't usually cook at home. I tried, but every time I cooked it was a disaster!

Florence: What did you do? Did you learn to cook?

Rochelle: No, I didn't. One of the people in my flat was an amazing cook. He was from Italy and he cooked great food for all of us.

Florence: Lucky you!

Track 137

/d/ closed, cleaned, enjoyed
/t/ cooked, asked, finished, liked, talked, walked
/Id/ invited, needed, started, wanted

Track 138

A: Where did you go on holiday?
B: I travelled around Europe for three weeks.
A: That sounds fun! Which place did you like the most?
B: I loved Italy. We stayed there for a week. We visited Venice and Rome
A: I went to Rome last year. I really enjoyed it. Did you speak Italian when you were there?
B: I tried. I asked for directions one day, but I didn't understand the answer!
A: Ha! I was the same. Did you like Venice?
B: It was very beautiful, but I didn't like the weather. It rained for two days!

Track 139

1
A: Hi Sam! What did you do at the weekend?
B: I was with Jo. We saw the new Tom Cruise film at the cinema.
A: How was it?
B: It was OK. The special effects were good, and some parts were exciting, but the story wasn't very good.

2
A: You look tired Beth. What did you do last night?
B: I went out for dinner with Jack.
A: Where did you go?
B: We went to the new Turkish restaurant in the town centre.
A: How was it?
B: It was fantastic! The food tasted amazing and it was quite cheap. You would love it.

3
A: Hi Nicki! So, did you see Mark's band play at the weekend?
B: Yes, I did.
A: Did you enjoy it?
B: No. It was awful!
A: Really?! Oh, no! Why?
B: Mark rapped at one point!
A: Mark rapped?!
B: Yes! It wasn't very good.

4
A: I didn't see you on Friday, Paul. Where were you?
B: I went to Rob's 30th birthday party.
A: Did you have a good time?
B: Well, it was a bit boring at first, but then I met a girl. She was really funny and great to spend time with.
A: Oh, yeah? Did you get her phone number?
B: Yes, we're going on a date on Thursday!

Unit 12
Track 143

Josh Hi, I'm Josh. I'm a journalist and I'm looking at the topic of 'New Beginnings'. And I really want to hear from you. So, if you're ready for a change in your life, what do you want to do next? Maybe you want to move to a new country? Or maybe you're leaving school or university. It's an ending, but it's also a beginning.

Do you want to go to university again and do another degree?

Do you want to get a job in the city, find a house and move in with some friends?

Or do you want to go travelling – to Asia or Australia? Or do a French course and move to Paris?

Or do you want to get married and have children?

What's next for you and your friends? Write an article and send it to our email address. Go to our website for the … [fade]

Track 145

1 A: What are you going to do after university?
   B: I'm going to go travelling in Australia.
   A: What are you going to do there?
   B: I'm going to get a job in a hotel, but I'm not going to work all the time. I'm going to do a surfing course too.

2 A: What are you going to do next year?
   B: I'm going to buy a house.
   A: Where are you going to buy it?
   B: In Glasgow – so I'm going to move to Scotland.
   A: Why are you going to move there?
   B: My brother lives there. We're going to work together and he's going to help me start my own business.

Track 147

Living for the weekend!
We spoke to businessman, Ralph Packer, about his weekends.

Interviewer: What do you usually do at weekends?
Ralph: On Saturdays I get up late. I eat breakfast and I do my Spanish homework – I'm learning Spanish for work right now. After that I go to the gym or I run 15 kilometres – I'm training for a marathon at the moment. Then I have a shower and I meet friends for dinner. On Sundays I often go shopping or to the cinema.
Interviewer: What did you do last weekend?
Ralph: Last weekend was different. I went to Iceland with my best friend. We flew to Reykjavik and then we drove north to Stykkisholmur, a beautiful fishing town. We stayed there for three nights. We visited the volcano museum and we walked up a mountain. And we saw the Northern Lights. It was an amazing weekend.
Interviewer: What are you going to do next weekend?
Ralph: I'm really excited because I'm going to go to my brother's wedding! The wedding is in London, so I'm going to drive there after work on Friday. And I'm going to stay in a hotel for two nights. It's going to be so much fun – I'm going to see a lot of friends and family.

Track 149

1
Kelly: Hello, Jeff. Are you here for a meeting?
Jeff: Hello, Kelly. Yes, I am. How are you?
Kelly: I'm fine, thanks. Oh, this is Ed – he's in my team. Ed, this is Jeff.
Ed: Nice to meet you, Jeff.
Jeff: Nice to meet you, too. Oh, is that the time? Sorry, but I'm late for my meeting.
Kelly: OK. See you later, Jeff.
Jeff: Yes. It was really nice to meet you, Ed. I hope we meet again. Bye.

2
Noah: Hey, Lisa. How are you?
Lisa: Hi, Noah. I'm good, thanks. How are you?
Noah: Great. …Er … I'm going to go for a coffee. Do you want to come?
Lisa: Oh, sorry. I'm going to meet my sister in town.
Noah: Oh, OK. Well it was great to see you.
Lisa: Yeah. Let's meet up soon. Message me.
Noah: OK. See you.

Acknowledgements

Images

Cover 6.1 Shutterstock (Rawpixel.com), New York; **6.2** Shutterstock (2shrimpS), New York; **6.3** Shutterstock (Antonio Guillem), New York; **7.1** Shutterstock (michaeljung), New York; **8.1** Shutterstock (Daniel M Ernst), New York; **8.2** Shutterstock (petch one), New York; **8.2, 8.3, 8.4, 8.5** Shutterstock (Art Alex), New York; **8.3** Shutterstock (Filip Bjorkman), New York; **8.4** Shutterstock (Filip Bjorkman), New York; **8.5** Shutterstock (Robert Biedermann), New York; **8.6 - 8.13, 12.6 - 12.21** Shutterstock (Puwadol Jaturawutthichai), New York; **8.14** Shutterstock (fizkes), New York; **9.1** Shutterstock (Zigres), New York; **9.2** Shutterstock (mykeyruna), New York; **9.3** Shutterstock (Daniel M Ernst), New York; **9.4** Rodolfo Sassano / Alamy Stock Foto; **9.5** ZUMA Press, Inc. / Alamy Stock Foto; **10.1** Shutterstock (StockLite), New York; **10.2** Shutterstock (ALPA PROD), New York; **10.3** Shutterstock (Monkey Business Images), New York; **11.1** Shutterstock (goodluz), New York; **11.2** Shutterstock (Jacob Lund), New York; **12.1** Shutterstock (Prostock-studio), New York; **12.2** Shutterstock (Lukassek), New York; **12.3** Shutterstock (Air Images), New York; **12.4** Shutterstock (Helen Kramarenko), New York; **12.4** Shutterstock (Pitchayaarch Photography), New York; **13.1** Shutterstock (Vitalii Vitleo), New York; **13.2** Shutterstock (Tinseltown), New York; **13.3** Shutterstock (Tinseltown), New York; **13.4** Shutterstock (Denis Makarenko), New York; **13.5** Shutterstock (Oleksandr Osipov), New York; **13.6** Shutterstock (Oleksandr Osipov), New York; **13.7** Shutterstock (Roman Samborskyi), New York; **14.1 - 14.9** Shutterstock (Inspiring), New York; **14.2** Shutterstock (stockfour), New York; **14.10** Shutterstock (Dean Drobot), New York; **14.11** Shutterstock (AlexLMX), New York; **14.12** Shutterstock (The Toidi), New York; **15.1** Shutterstock (palomadelosrios), New York; **16.1** Shutterstock (Jacob Lund), New York; **16.2** Shutterstock (l i g h t p o e t), New York; **16.3** Shutterstock (Iakov Filimonov), New York; **16.4** Shutterstock (ZoranOrcik), New York; **16.5** Shutterstock (Monkey Business Images), New York; **17.1** Shutterstock (sirtravelalot), New York; **17.2** Shutterstock (GaudiLab), New York; **17.3** Shutterstock (Minerva Studio), New York; **17.4** Shutterstock (Andrey Arkusha), New York; **17.5** Shutterstock (Shymko Svitlana), New York; **17.6** Shutterstock (Vectorry), New York; **17.7** Shutterstock (Mascha Tace), New York; **17.8** Shutterstock (Sergey Mastepanov), New York; **17.9** Shutterstock (David Arts), New York; **17.10** Shutterstock (matrioshka), New York; **18.1** Shutterstock (Markus Pfaff), New York; **18.2** © James Magrane / Bagley Wood Productions; **18.3** © James Magrane / Bagley Wood Productions; **18.4** © James Magrane / Bagley Wood Productions; **18.5** © James Magrane / Bagley Wood Productions; **18.6** © James Magrane / Bagley Wood Productions; **18.7** Shutterstock (Daboost), New York; **18.8** Shutterstock (Christian Vinces), New York; **18.9** Shutterstock (stocker1970), New York; **18.10** Shutterstock (Tooykrub), New York; **18.11** Shutterstock (emperorcosar), New York; **20.1** Shutterstock (KREUS), New York; **20.2** Shutterstock (Paul_K), New York; **20.3** Shutterstock (Perfect Vectors), New York; **20.4** Shutterstock (Ogovorka), New York; **20.5** Shutterstock (Andrew Angelov), New York; **20.6** Shutterstock (prapann), New York; **20.7** Shutterstock (LiveVector), New York; **20.8** Shutterstock (Pixel Embargo), New York; **20.9** Shutterstock (maroke), New York; **20.10** Shutterstock (Yeti studio), New York; **20.11** Shutterstock (burnel1), New York; **20.12** Shutterstock (Pakhnyushchy), New York; **20.13** Shutterstock (Photoongraphy), New York; **20.14** Shutterstock (Mikhail Turov), New York; **21.1** Shutterstock (Artos), New York; **21.1** Shutterstock (blackzheep), New York; **21.2** Shutterstock (Rawpixel.com), New York; **21.3** Shutterstock (stocker1970), New York; **21.4** Shutterstock (MEzairi), New York; **21.5** Shutterstock (rawmn), New York; **21.6** Shutterstock (Mistervlad), New York; **21.7** Shutterstock (Africa Studio), New York; **21.8** Shutterstock (Yannick Morelli), New York; **21.9** Shutterstock (Rawpixel.com), New York; **21.10** Shutterstock (EZ-Stock Studio), New York; **21.11** Shutterstock (Billion Photos), New York; **21.12** Shutterstock (Nigel Stripe), New York; **21.13** Shutterstock (Teerasak Ladnongkhun), New York; **21.14** Shutterstock (Image Republic), New York; **21.15** Shutterstock (BigPixel Photo), New York; **21.16** Shutterstock (Aldeca Productions), New York; **21.17** Shutterstock (Africa Studio), New York; **21.18** Shutterstock (Igisheva Maria), New York; **22.1** Shutterstock (xiaorui), New York; **22.2** Shutterstock (Tarzhanova), New York; **22.3** Shutterstock (Yummyphotos), New York; **22.4** Shutterstock (vitaliy_73), New York; **22.5** Shutterstock (TheGlowingCarrot), New York; **22.6** Shutterstock (Artem Avetisyan), New York; **22.7** Shutterstock (DenisProduction.com), New York; **22.8** Shutterstock (Kapitula Olga), New York; **22.9** Shutterstock (Magdalena Wielobob), New York; **22.10** Shutterstock (DenisProduction.com), New York; **22.11** Shutterstock (iamtui7), New York; **22.12** Shutterstock (Dean Drobot), New York; **22.13** Shutterstock (kikovic), New York; **22.14** Shutterstock (Jelena Zelen), New York; **24.1** Shutterstock (icsnaps), New York; **24.2** Shutterstock (MPanchenko), New York; **24.3** Shutterstock (M Kunz), New York; **24.4** Shutterstock (Anton_Ivanov), New York; **24.5** Shutterstock (magicoven), New York; **24.6** Shutterstock (Mikhaylovskiy), New York; **24.6** Shutterstock (Graeme Scott), New York; **24.7** Shutterstock (Anna_Pustynnikova), New York; **24.8** Shutterstock (stockcreations), New York; **24.9** Shutterstock (stockcreations), New York; **24.10** Shutterstock (New Africa), New York; **24.11** Shutterstock (Tarasyuk Igor), New York; **24.12** Shutterstock (Nitr), New York; **24.13** Shutterstock (Africa Studio), New York; **25.1** Shutterstock (JivkoM), New York; **25.2** Shutterstock (Razym), New York; **25.3** Shutterstock (michaeljung), New York; **26.1** Shutterstock (Studio Peace), New York; **26.2** Shutterstock (aastock), New York; **26.3** Shutterstock (Studio Peace), New York; **26.4** Shutterstock (Olena Yakobchuk), New York; **26.5** Shutterstock (Olena Yakobchuk), New York; **26.6** Shutterstock (Alemon cz), New York; **26.7** Shutterstock (rasskazov), New York; **27.1** Shutterstock (Ranta Images), New York; **27.2** Shutterstock (Rawpixel.com), New York; **27.3** Shutterstock (Arvind Balaraman), New York; **27.4** Shutterstock (Ami Parikh), New York; **28.1** Shutterstock (1000 Words), New York; **28.2** Shutterstock (I Wei Huang), New York; **28.3** Shutterstock (Vadym Lavra), New York; **28.4** Shutterstock (phaustov), New York; **28.5** Shutterstock (Kyryk Ivan), New York; **28.6** Shutterstock (Dan Rentea), New York; **29.1** Shutterstock (Impact Photography), New York; **30.1 - 30.12** Shutterstock (Iurii Kachkovskyi), New York; **31.1** Shutterstock (Lia Koltyrina), New York; **31.2** Shutterstock (Lia Koltyrina), New York; **31.3** Shutterstock (Lia Koltyrina), New York; **31.4** Shutterstock (aastock), New York; **32.1** Shutterstock (Ihnatovich Maryia), New York; **32.2** Shutterstock (Fotoluminate LLC), New York; **32.3** Shutterstock (pixelheadphoto digitalskillet), New York; **32.4** Shutterstock (Daniel M Ernst), New York; **32.5** Shutterstock (Sam Wordley), New York; **34.1** Shutterstock (El Nariz), New York; **34.2** Shutterstock (Africa Studio), New York; **34.3** Shutterstock (Aleksandar Todorovic), New York; **34.4** Shutterstock (Kamil Macniak), New York; **34.5** Shutterstock (Dean Drobot), New York; **34.6** Shutterstock (Standret), New York; **34.7** Shutterstock (Rido), New York; **34.8** Shutterstock (Monkey Business Images), New York; **34.9** Shutterstock (Dean Drobot), New York; **34.10** Shutterstock (Maxisport), New York; **34.11** Shutterstock (anatoliy_gleb), New York; **34.12** Shutterstock (Pavel L Photo and Video), New York; **34.13** Shutterstock (Izf), New York; **34.14** Shutterstock (Microgen), New York; **35.1** Shutterstock (Dragon Images), New York; **35.2** Shutterstock (Antonio Guillem), New York; **36.1** Shutterstock (frantic00), New York; **36.2** Shutterstock (Success media), New York; **36.3** Shutterstock (Friends Stock), New York; **36.4** Shutterstock (Patrizia Tilly), New York; **37.1** Shutterstock (Halfpoint), New York; **37.2** Shutterstock (Izabela Magier), New York; **37.3** Shutterstock (Africa Studio), New York; **37.4** Shutterstock (Luis Molinero), New York; **37.5** Shutterstock (BELL KA PANG), New York; **37.6** Shutterstock (Stokkete), New York; **37.7** Shutterstock (Andrii Kobryn), New York; **37.8** Shutterstock (PThira89), New York; **37.9** Shutterstock (Dmytro Zinkevych), New York; **37.10** Shutterstock (Jihan Nafiaa Zahri), New York; **38.1** Shutterstock (G-Stock Studio), New York; **38.2** Shutterstock (Monkey Business Images), New York; **38.3** Shutterstock (Andrey_Popov), New York; **38.4** Shutterstock (Photographee.eu), New York; **39.1** Shutterstock (Monkey Business Images), New York; **39.2** Shutterstock (Halfpoint), New York; **40.1** Shutterstock (Sergey Tarasov), New York; **40.2** Shutterstock (Monkey Business Images), New York;

40.3 Shutterstock (Protasov AN), New York; **40.4** Shutterstock (Cozy Home), New York; **40.5** Shutterstock (Blazej Lyjak), New York; **40.6** Shutterstock (Undrey), New York; **40.7** Shutterstock (noreefly), New York; **40.8** Shutterstock (New Africa), New York; **41.1** Shutterstock (antoniodiaz), New York; **42.1** Shutterstock (phM2019), New York; **42.2** Shutterstock (kei907), New York; **42.3** Shutterstock (Kreminska), New York; **42.4** Shutterstock (Dusan Petkovic), New York; **42.5** Shutterstock (Africa Studio), New York; **42.6** Shutterstock (Ron Adar), New York; **42.7** Shutterstock (DFree), New York; **42.8** Shutterstock (DFree), New York; **42.9** Matthew Horwood / Alamy Stock Foto; **43.1** Shutterstock (lunopark), New York; **44.1** Shutterstock (Goskova Tatiana), New York; **44.2** Shutterstock (Yuliya Yesina), New York; **44.3** Shutterstock (goffkein.pro), New York; **44.4** Shutterstock (Edvard Nalbantjan), New York; **44.5** Shutterstock (A_stockphoto), New York; **44.6** Shutterstock (GingerKitten), New York; **44.7** Shutterstock (GingerKitten), New York; **45.1** Shutterstock (Djomas), New York; **45.2** Shutterstock (Moremar), New York; **45.3** Shutterstock (Gergely Zsolnai), New York; **46.1** Shutterstock (oneinchpunch), New York; **46.2** Shutterstock (nampix), New York; **46.3** Shutterstock (Kolonko), New York; **48.1** Shutterstock (Trendsetter Images), New York; **48.2** Shutterstock (Nomad_Soul), New York; **48.3** Shutterstock (Prostock-studio), New York; **48.4** Shutterstock (Catarina Belova), New York; **48.5** Shutterstock (Monkey Business Images), New York; **48.6** Shutterstock (TORWAISTUDIO), New York; **48.7** Shutterstock (Olga Danylenko), New York; **48.8** Shutterstock (oneinchpunch), New York; **48.9** Shutterstock (View Apart), New York; **48.10** Shutterstock (mavo), New York; **48.11** Shutterstock (Monkey Business Images), New York; **48.12** Shutterstock (AJR_photo), New York; **48.13** Shutterstock (Monkey Business Images), New York; **48.14** Shutterstock (Kleber Cordeiro), New York; **50.1** Shutterstock (sondem), New York; **50.2** Shutterstock (furtseff), New York; **52.1** Shutterstock (Makistock), New York; **52.2** Shutterstock (Michael715), New York; **52.3** Shutterstock (dennizn), New York; **52.4** Shutterstock (K3S), New York; **52.5** Shutterstock (Solarisys), New York; **53.1** Shutterstock (maxpro), New York; **53.2** Shutterstock (kan_chana), New York; **53.3** Shutterstock (REDPIXEL.PL), New York; **53.4** Shutterstock (Jack Frog), New York; **53.5** Shutterstock (Africa Studio), New York; **53.6** Shutterstock (oneinchpunch), New York; **54.1** Shutterstock (Markus Mainka), New York; **54.2** Shutterstock (Marina Bakush), New York; **54.3** Shutterstock (Marian Weyo), New York; **54.4** Shutterstock (Africa Studio), New York; **54.5** Shutterstock (New Africa), New York; **54.6** Shutterstock (Evgeny Karandaev), New York; **54.7** Shutterstock (5 second Studio), New York; **54.8** Shutterstock (Sea Wave), New York; **54.9** Shutterstock (minicase), New York; **54.10** Shutterstock (Brent Hofacker), New York; **54.11** Shutterstock (vitals), New York; **54.12** Shutterstock (Zoeytoja), New York; **54.13** Shutterstock (Larisa Blinova), New York; **54.14** Shutterstock (eugenegurkov), New York; **54.15** Shutterstock (Lyubimova Tatiana), New York; **54.16** Shutterstock (Martin Gaal), New York; **54.17** Shutterstock (Eugenia Lucasenco), New York; **54.18** Shutterstock (Noppadon stocker), New York; **54.19** Shutterstock (beats1), New York; **54.20** Shutterstock (Eugenia Lucasenco), New York; **54.21** Shutterstock (Dmytro Zinkevych), New York; **55.1** Shutterstock (nexus 7), New York; **55.2** Shutterstock (ER_09), New York; **55.3** Shutterstock (topseller), New York; **55.5** Shutterstock (Matt Kay), New York; **55.6** Shutterstock (BAKOUNINE), New York; **55.7** Shutterstock (ComposedPix), New York; **55.8** Shutterstock (360b), New York; **55.9** Shutterstock (lev radin), New York; **55.10** Shutterstock (Bart Lenoir), New York; **56.1** Shutterstock (greenland), New York; **56.2** Shutterstock (pio3), New York; **56.3** Shutterstock (Master1305), New York; **56.4** Shutterstock (mavo), New York; **56.4** Shutterstock (Bill45), New York; **56.5** Shutterstock (Denis Val), New York; **56.6** Shutterstock (Africa Studio), New York; **56.7** Shutterstock (MillaF), New York; **56.8** Shutterstock (Monkey Business Images), New York; **56.9** Shutterstock (RossHelen), New York; **56.10** Shutterstock (RossHelen), New York; **56.11** Shutterstock (Claudio Divizia), New York; **57.1** Shutterstock (Skully), New York; **57.2** Shutterstock (Haali), New York; **58.1** Shutterstock (GoodStudio), New York; **58.2** Shutterstock (Kzenon), New York; **59.1** Shutterstock (Astrovector), New York; **59.2** Shutterstock (Flamingo Images), New York; **59.3** Shutterstock (fizkes), New York; **60.1** Shutterstock (AS photo studio), New York; **60.2** Shutterstock (Yulia Grigoryeva), New York; **60.3** Shutterstock (Hadrian), New York; **60.4** Shutterstock (Francesco Bonino), New York; **60.5** Shutterstock (Tana888), New York; **62.1** Shutterstock (Roman Samborskyi), New York; **62.2** Shutterstock (Kaspars Grinvalds), New York; **62.3** Shutterstock (Makistock), New York; **62.4** Shutterstock (Dean Drobot), New York; **62.5** Shutterstock (New Africa), New York; **62.6** Shutterstock (Ollyy), New York; **62.7** Shutterstock (bbernard), New York; **62.8** Shutterstock (Syda Productions), New York; **63.2** Shutterstock (cosmic_fellow), New York; **64.1** Shutterstock (Andrew Roland), New York; **64.2** Shutterstock (S-F), New York; **64.3** Shutterstock (nikolpetr), New York; **64.4** Shutterstock (Dmitry Naumov), New York; **64.5** Shutterstock (Alliance Images), New York; **64.6** Shutterstock (Duncan Andison), New York; **64.7** Shutterstock (gorillaimages), New York; **64.8** Shutterstock (Simev), New York; **64.9** Shutterstock (Willy Barton), New York; **64.10** Shutterstock (Andrew Lever), New York; **64.11** Shutterstock (Dmytro Vietrov), New York; **64.12** Shutterstock (SNeG17), New York; **65.1** Shutterstock (r.nagy), New York; **65.2** Shutterstock (Capricorn Studio), New York; **65.3** Shutterstock (Matva), New York; **66.1** Shutterstock (Lewis Tse Pui Lung), New York; **66.2** Shutterstock (Mangostar), New York; **66.3** Shutterstock (Monkey Business Images), New York; **67.1** Shutterstock (emojoez), New York; **67.2** Shutterstock (Brian A Jackson), New York; **67.3** Shutterstock (Roman Samborskyi), New York; **67.4** Shutterstock (thodonal88), New York; **67.5** Shutterstock (Maria Sbytova), New York; **67.6** Shutterstock (Iryna Inshyna), New York; **68.1** Shutterstock (Photographee.eu), New York; **68.2** Shutterstock (Andrey tiyk), New York; **68.3** Shutterstock (Archi_Viz), New York; **68.4** Shutterstock (Photographee.eu), New York; **68.5** Shutterstock (Photographee.eu), New York; **68.6** Shutterstock (Photographee.eu), New York; **68.7** Shutterstock (ben bryant), New York; **68.8** Shutterstock (David Papazian), New York; **68.9** Shutterstock (New Africa), New York; **68.10** Shutterstock (Orientaly), New York; **68.11** Shutterstock (Neirfy), New York; **68.12** Shutterstock (bbgreg), New York; **69.1** Shutterstock (Jacob Lund), New York; **69.2** Shutterstock (vulcano), New York; **70.1** Shutterstock (HABRDA), New York; **70.2** Shutterstock (Steve Design), New York; **70.3** Shutterstock (Dmitri Mehh), New York; **70.4** Shutterstock (arturasker), New York; **70.5** Shutterstock (izas), New York; **70.6** Shutterstock (ESB Professional), New York; **70.7** Shutterstock (alice-photo), New York; **70.8** Shutterstock (crystal51), New York; **70.9** Shutterstock (1000 Words), New York; **71.1** Shutterstock (Monkey Business Images), New York; **71.2** Shutterstock (Prostock-studio), New York; **73.1** Shutterstock (Photographee.eu), New York; **73.2** Shutterstock (Willy Barton), New York; **74.1** Shutterstock (Aleksandr Ozerov), New York; **74.2** Shutterstock (Statia Grossman), New York; **74.3** Shutterstock (Alberto Loyo), New York; **76.1** Shutterstock (Katia Seniutina), New York; **78.1** Shutterstock (f11photo), New York; **78.2** Shutterstock (Parrot Ivan), New York; **78.3** Shutterstock (Sean Pavone), New York; **79.1** Shutterstock (Monkey Business Images), New York; **79.2** Shutterstock (michaeljung), New York; **79.3** Shutterstock (4045), New York; **79.4** Shutterstock (Pefkos), New York; **79.5** Shutterstock (Antonio Guillem), New York; **79.6** Shutterstock (Nor Gal), New York; **79.7** Shutterstock (Andrey_Popov), New York; **80.1** Shutterstock (Shift Drive), New York; **80.2** Shutterstock (Monkey Business Images), New York; **80.3** Shutterstock (Monkey Business Images), New York; **80.4** Shutterstock (Devo Satria Ichwaldi), New York; **81.1** Shutterstock (yaichatchai), New York; **81.2** Shutterstock (Rauf Aliyev), New York; **81.3** Shutterstock (riobi), New York; **82.1** Shutterstock (lassedesignen), New York; **82.2** Shutterstock (fotoinfot), New York; **83.1** Shutterstock (Krakenimages), New York; **83.2** Shutterstock (PR Image Factory), New York; **83.3** Shutterstock (nata_nytiaga), New York; **83.4** Shutterstock (Rawpixel.com), New York; **83.5** Shutterstock (Capricorn Studio), New York; **84.1** Shutterstock (xtock), New York; **84.2** Shutterstock (Syda Productions), New York; **84.3** Shutterstock (dfrolovXIII), New York; **84.4** Shutterstock (Mihai_Andritoiu), New

York; **85.1** Shutterstock (Pavlo Plakhotia), New York; **85.2 - 85.7** Shutterstock (Chaim Devine), New York; **86.1** Shutterstock (mayrum), New York; **86.2** Shutterstock (Rawpixel.com), New York; **86.3** Shutterstock (Life_imageS), New York; **87.1** Shutterstock (oneinchpunch), New York; **87.2** Shutterstock (Olga Klochanko), New York; **88.1** Shutterstock (S_Photo), New York; **88.2** Shutterstock (Travelerpix), New York; **88.3** Shutterstock (Rido), New York; **88.4** Shutterstock (Eugenio Marongiu), New York; **88.5** Shutterstock (Zoran Zeremski), New York; **88.6** Shutterstock (Rawpixel.com), New York; **98.1, 102.1.1** Shutterstock (Jimmie48 Photography), New York; **98.2, 102.2.2** Shutterstock (Andrea Raffin), New York; **98.3, 102.3.3** Shutterstock (Featureflash Photo Agency), New York; **98.4, 102.4.4** Shutterstock (Kathy Hutchins), New York; **98.5, 102.5.5** Shutterstock (Asatur Yesayants), New York; **98.6, 102.6.6** Shutterstock (Tinseltown), New York; **98.7, 102.7.7** Shutterstock (Kathy Hutchins), New York; **99.4** Shutterstock (Kamil Macniak), New York; **100.1** Shutterstock (MikaHolanda), New York; **100.2** Shutterstock (prochasson frederic), New York; **101.1** Shutterstock (Roop_Dey), New York; **101.2** Shutterstock (William Perugini), New York; **103.5** Shutterstock (Africa Studio), New York; **104.1** Shutterstock (kurhan), New York; **104.2** Shutterstock (Antonio Guillem), New York; **105.1** Shutterstock (KAZLOVA IRYNA), New York; **105.2** Shutterstock (adriaticfoto), New York

Illustrations

23, 28, 72, 99, 103 Seb Camagajevac (Beehive Illustrations)

63 Ilias Arahovitis (Beehive Illustrations

49, 58, 81, 89 Wild Apple Design Ltd.

Authors' acknowledgements

We would like to thank our editors and all the team at Delta/Klett for believing in our vision and helping us to shape it into coursebooks that we can be truly proud of.

We'd particularly like to thank editors Sheila Dignen, Richard Storton, and Anna Gunn, as well as our excellent Teacher's Book author, Thomas Hadland for their support, advice and professionalism.

Our excellent designers at Wild Apple also deserve special mention. Their creativity, enthusiasm and patience have helped us create beautiful books that bring the words on the page to life.

Special mention also to our audio producer, Jeff Capel. His good humour and fantastic directing skills resulted in clear, yet authentic-sounding audio tracks. And of course, additional thanks to our video producer, James Magrane, who crafted engaging video clips and braved the British weather to film our vox pops.

We'd also like to thank our children, Ruby and Lenny, for their patience with their irritable parents during the intense writing phases of the course!

The publishers would also like to thank the following teachers for their help in developing the course: Liz Foody and Sarah Walker.

About the authors

Cathy and Louis Rogers are a husband-and-wife author team. They met back in 2002, whilst teaching at the same language school in Cologne, Germany. Here's some more information about them:

Cathy Rogers

After graduating from Cardiff University with a degree in English Literature and German, Cathy had a brief career in customer services at a wine company, and then at a pharmaceutical company with customers in both the UK and Germany.

She then took a TEFL course and moved to Cologne, in Germany, where she taught business English and met fellow-teacher, Louis. They then moved to Portugal together and taught general English at a language school in Lisbon. After a year there, an opportunity arose in Cologne, so they returned to Germany and moved back into teaching business English.

They then decided to further their careers by gaining extra qualifications and so both did a masters in ELT at Nottingham Trent University. During this time, they also taught EAP to International students. After completing the MA, Cathy moved into Materials Development and worked in ELT publishing.

She lives in Reading with Louis, their two children and their cat. She now works full time on materials creation, and teaches general English on a voluntary basis through an Oxford-based charity. In her spare time she enjoys running and has recently completed her first half-marathon.

Louis Rogers

While studying for a degree in Marketing and English Language Studies, Louis also completed a Trinity Certificate in TESOL and taught in UK language schools for a couple of summers. After graduating, Louis moved immediately to Sicily, in Italy, for his first full-time teaching post. Here he taught general English to teenagers and adults.

In 2001 Louis moved to Cologne, Germany, where he taught business English. His next job was teaching general English in Lisbon, Portugal, followed by a return to Cologne and more business English.

In 2005 he returned to the UK and completed an MA in ELT at Nottingham Trent University, teaching EAP to International students alongside studying. After completing the MA, Louis taught international students for over a decade at the University of Reading. While teaching at the University of Reading, Louis began to write materials for a range of publishers. To date he has authored or co-authored over 50 titles in ELT.

He lives in Reading with his wife, Cathy and their two children, plus the family cat, Rosie. In his spare time he enjoys playing football, coaching kids' football and gardening.